The Ultimate Guide To Nutritional Supplement Advertising

How To Write Sales-Boosting, Control-Busting Supplement Ads

By Callum Birch

I0462334

"(General advertising) is like casting bread upon the waters and hoping for its return." Claude Hopkins, Scientific Advertising.

Table of Contents

Preface

Have you heard the old story about a motorist caught in dense fog?

He couldn't see a thing, so he followed the tail light of the car in front. He stayed very close to this car, afraid of losing the guiding light and having to navigate on his own.

Suddenly, the car in front of him stopped very quickly, and they crashed.

Enraged, the driver jumped out and yelled, "why didn't you warn me you were going to stop?!"

"Why should I?" the man replied. "I'm in my own garage."

Here's the point: following and modeling others can be an efficient and profitable strategy, but…

Only If You Choose The Right Model!

When it comes to marketing, most small businesses emulate big brand-name companies… and spend (waste) a lot of money on image, brand and presence.

The problem is, these big companies have 101 reasons to advertise the way they do. They want to please their board of directors, appease their stockholders, look good to Wall Street, present themselves well in the eyes of the media, build brand identity, and win advertising awards. Right at the very bottom of that list: *getting customers.*

The main concern for most small businesses, however, is exactly that: getting enough customers to pay the bills and, sometimes, to grow. So, allow me to introduce you to a radical idea…

Everything You See Big Brand-Name Companies Doing Is The Exact Opposite Of What Works For Small Business.

Here is what I mean. Most corporations outsource their advertising to agencies. Several agencies compete for the account. Whoever wins gets to spend the client's budget for the period of the contract.

If sales go up whilst the advertising runs, the agency is celebrated. If sales go down, the agency is fired. And, the cycle continues.

The problem is, the link between their advertising and sales is weak at best. They have no idea whether an ad produced any sales at all, let alone how many. If sales rise, it could be due to any number of factors. So, there's no way to know whether the advertising was effective or not.

It's very expensive and wasteful.

As I said, these companies have lots of priorities over and above getting customers and making sales. Throwing money at advertising without a return is not an issue; they have the resources to absorb the expense. And, perhaps they hope to get their money back in a future sale or an increase in share price. I don't know. But what I do know is this: small and even medium-sized businesses do NOT have money to waste on unprofitable advertising.

For them, the purpose of advertising is to make sales. Not to satisfy some creative whim or stroke a man's ego...

To make SALES.

Damn it! I promised myself I wouldn't ramble on about how terrible most marketing and advertising is. But hey, at least I've got it out of the way early on. And the reason I bought this up in the first place is that...

This book is for small to medium sized businesses, who sell nutritional supplements, and want MEASURABLE RESULTS.

It's for owners, presidents, marketing directors and copywriters who want to use direct response advertising to generate sales.

Specifically, you will find a roadmap for producing an effective nutritional supplement advertisement— whether that's an online sales page, sales letter, space ad, magalog or something else.

Everything you will learn can be applied to any format, any media type, any market, and any product.

Therefore, from this point forward I will refer to the different types of advertising collectively as "ad".

Righty-o! Here's a roadmap for the journey you are about to embark upon:

Part I — Advertising Foundations

The first part of this book is about little-known advertising principles that can transform your business.

Part II — Preparing Your Ad

How to gather everything you need to write a profitable ad.

Part III — Writing Your Ad

How to find your big idea, write a stand-out headline, hook your prospect so they can't stop reading, and more.

Part IV — Editing Your Ad

A step-by-step process for editing, designing and testing your copy (at no cost).

Part V — FTC/FDA Compliance

Guidelines to make sure your ad is both effective... and... complies with FTC and FDA regulations.

Part V1 — Resources

Finally, a list of books, websites and other resources you can use to further your ability to write effective nutritional supplement ads.

Okay… Strap in, and enjoy the ride!

PART I:

ADVERTISING

FOUNDATIONS

One Question To Solve All Your Advertising Problems

Imagine two different salesmen walking down the street.

One goes from door to door and talks to people, makes his pitch, and asks for an order. If what he's doing is working, his pockets will be stuffed full of cash and orders by the end of the day. If not, his pockets will be bare, and he'll know that he failed.

The other salesman walks along the pavement, shouting out his pitch to every house he passes. He will never know if what he is saying is having any effect. At the end of the day, he couldn't tell you if he earned a single new customer.

Why am I telling you this story?

Because every business needs customers to survive. And to get customers it needs to sell. Yet, most business people have no idea that advertising is nothing more than…

Salesmanship Multiplied By A Mass Medium.

A single ad does the job of dozens of individual salesmen. But most ads neglect salesmanship altogether. They're like the guy that shouts his pitch at every house. They effectively say, "Hey, I've entertained you, so won't you go find my product or service and buy it?" … and the advertiser has no idea whether or not it produced sales.

Okay, here's how you can apply this to maximize your advertising returns.

When you are faced with a question or decision about an ad, ask yourself:

"Would this help a salesman sell the product if he were sitting face-to-face with a prospect?"

Do you see the power in asking this question? It cuts right through the B.S. and goes direct to the heart of the matter. It holds no regard for personal desires. It holds no regard for the opinion of anybody else who believe they know what the ad should include. (Remember, most of the world is blissfully unaware of what makes an effective ad—so be careful who you listen to).

In fact, nobody can say anything about whether your ad will be successful until you test the market's response. But you can, and should, maximize your chances of success by following the unvarying laws of advertising.

And, this question gives you the power to apply the most important principle of all: that advertising is salesmanship multiplied by a mass medium.

For example, should you use a fancy font to get the prospect's attention? Well, using this technique, the next question you might ask is:

"Would wearing a fancy suit make a salesman more likely to sell your product if sat face-to-face with a prospect?"

Maybe. Maybe not. If you were selling to a farmer, it might make the prospect feel as though you were talking down to them. Or, at least, he might struggle to identify with you. And as the old sales adage goes: we only buy from those we know, like and trust. So, in this case, the suit would harm your ability to sell.

If you were selling to a high-powered lawyer, on the other hand, who expected a well-dressed business associate, then wearing the suit would surely help your case.

But here's the kicker: in either case, the way you dress is secondary to what you are selling. Suit or not, nobody will buy your product if they do not have a burning pain... if your product is not a solution to that pain... and if you don't persuade them that they should invest in your solution right now.

If a desperate drug addict found a dealer who offered him the first shot of heroin for free, would he care if the guy was wearing a t-shirt and shorts? I doubt it. He'd just want the damn heroin—a solution to his problem, "risk-free."

Similarly, the manner in which you dress a salesman—or its multiplied form: an advertisement—is of little consequence.

Okay, here are some more examples:

Question: "Should I include an image in my ad?"

Answer: If a salesman had five minutes or less to make the sale, would using the time to show the prospect an image help or hinder the sale?

Question: "How long should the copy in my ad be?"

Answer: How much time would a salesman need to develop trust, fill a burning need, and help the prospect justify the expense?

Anyway, I'm sure you get the idea.

And, if you take anything at all away from this book... if you remember just one nugget of information... please, please, please make it this.

It really does give you the power to solve any advertising problem, and avoid being led astray by misinformed colleagues, friends and family.

Advertising Secrets Of The Greatest Showman

Have you ever seen the movie, "The Greatest Showman"?

It's a blockbuster about the life and work of P.T. Barnum, the circus man who made, lost, and re-made a fortune by tapping into the power of sensationalism.

There was the bearded lady…

The one-horned goat billed as a unicorn …

The man with three legs…

A lady with exceptional strength…

… and the "wolf-man" with excessive facial hair.

You know, great advertising has more to do with P.T. Barnum than any of the ads you see during the commercials of the Super Bowl or Saturday night TV.

Barnum was a man of the people who understood psychology and what makes people tick. In fact, he created such an urgent sense of curiosity that crowds fought to hand over their hard-earned cash for a ticket to his shows.

Whatever You Think Of Barnum Profiting From The Unusual Appearance Of Others, He Was… Without Doubt… A Master Salesman!

So, how does this apply to writing copy for nutritional supplement promotions? It's simple: advertising is salesmanship multiplied by a mass medium.

Therefore, the ad you write to sell your product (or your client's product) must be a master salesman-in-print.

Here is what the master salesman knows that big brand-name companies and ad agencies do not.

First, he knows why people do NOT buy. People do not buy because they like your logo or the design of your website. They do not buy because you're funny or clever with your words. They do not buy because you claim to be the best in the world. And, they do not buy because you have a great product.

The master salesman knows that people only buy from him when he empathizes with their pain, develops trust, makes them an offer to solve their problem that no sane person could refuse, and helps them justify the expense.

He understands just how critical it is to get them to act on his offer IMMEDIATELY. And as P.T. Barnum proved, consumers pay to satisfy their curiosity. It is almost never the product itself that people buy....

It's the aura, the myth, the promises and the dreams that surround it!

What Every Profitable Advertisement Has In Common

In his book, Scientific Advertising, Claude Hopkins (the greatest ad man of all time) shared a story from his childhood.

He recalled a small stream near his home. This stream turned a wooden wheel, and the wheel powered a mill.

Then one day, somebody decided to install a turbine and dynamos. With no additional water or power, the same stream then ran a manufacturing plant.

The point is, there had been an enormous amount of wasted power in that small stream, and similarly…

There Is Enormous Wasted Power In Advertising!

Business people run unprofitable ads year after year. There are ads that cost $100 that could be replaced by a $5 ad and generate higher returns. And, these underpowered and utterly unprofitable ads all have one thing in common:

They Are Not "Keyed", Tested, Or Traced.

The advertiser has no idea whether their ad is generating sales. And in all likelihood, it isn't, because no-one knows enough people to average up the desires of the market. They can't possibly, therefore, determine the markets' response to any ad without measuring response. But still, the businessman keeps spending on untraced ads.

Why? I don't know. But if you were to push me for an answer, I'd say it's for one of two reasons:

1. They don't know HOW to create effective advertising, or

2. They are deliberately ignoring the laws of advertising, and sacrificing sales, to satisfy some desire.

It's a pity because almost any advertising question can be answered cheaply, quickly and absolutely using a test campaign.

And you can get a statically-significant result in a split test by mailing each piece to as little as 2000 names.

You can test new markets and new products. You can test new methods of selling products that are already advertised successfully.

Headlines, guarantees, offers, USP's, price, appeals, layout. They can all be improved. And even if you only bump response by a fraction…

… the extra sales will go DIRECTLY on your bottom line.

But here's where the real power of testing comes in… When you know what it costs to acquire 1000 customers, you know what it will cost to acquire 1 million.

Which means you can spend small amounts of money to test your assumptions, find a hot market, hot product, and hot copy… and PROVE that it's safe to invest larger sums in expanding your empire.

You know the story behind McDonald's, don't you?

It all started in 1952 when Ray Kroc walked into a hamburger stand in California to sell the two brothers who owned it—Mac and Jim MacDonald—a milkshake machine. Kroc noticed that the hamburgers were being produced quickly, efficiently and inexpensively. And, he managed to convince the two brothers to let him franchise their method. Forty years later, McDonald's is a $40-billion-a-year business. But…

It All Started By Perfecting The Method On A Tiny Scale!

And that's the best way to approach advertising. Test with a small but statistically-significant number of people until it's profitable… then scale up.

Best way to make your ads traceable so you can test results?

Offline, use a department number in the address. If the ad is going out to different lists or media, give each one a different department number. This allows you to track the results for each location, media, time or year... everything.

Online? Well, I don't even know where to start... there are thousands of tools you could use. If anything, the challenge is knowing WHAT to measure. If you are already testing advertising results effectively then you already know how to do this. If not, then I'd recommend keeping it very simple. Stick to measuring a few key metrics and remember to stay focused on the big picture: money in versus money out.

Fundamental Rules Of Selling

You know, scientific evidence is really important for nutritional supplement promotions. It helps you make your claims believable and legal (which keeps the FTC of your case). But... If you use science in the wrong place or in the wrong way, it can kill your response and turn an otherwise great promotion into a complete flop.

Why? Because of the three fundamental rules of selling:

1. People don't like the idea of being sold

2. People buy things for emotional, not rational, reasons

3. Once sold, people need to satisfy their emotional decisions with logic.

Using scientific evidence is about as rational as you can be. And rule number two states that people buy for emotional, not rational reasons. So, if you use science too early—before the reader has made an emotional decision to buy—then you'll lose them.

The solution to this is simple: your lead should ALWAYS be emotional, followed by scientific evidence and other logic to prove your claims later on. And...

This Lesson Is Even More Important If You Are A Man!

You see, men can only identify a handful of emotional states (and often confuse "being hungry" and "being tired" as emotions). So, they tend to write feature-heavy copy that talks about the size, performance and expense of the thing.

Research has found, though, that women have something like 200 identifiable emotions. Feeling "appreciated" carries different emotional weight than feeling "loved" or "adored".

Therefore, women tend to naturally write about the benefits and the "quality" of whatever they are selling… about how it feels to experience the thing. Women, therefore, are usually better at writing emotional copy. It can take some extra work for us blokes to write an ad that resonates with women!

Okay, so what if you are writing to a predominantly male market? Well, most health markets are female-dominated. Not all, but most. And, it's really irrelevant, because…

Women Control 90% Of All Buying Decisions!

"A man has two reasons for buying anything. The reason he tells his wife… and the real reason." — Mark Twain

Yep, even if you are writing to a bloke a woman often makes the ultimate buying decision. In fact, your prospect may even hand your sales letter (physical or digital) to his partner... so... your letter has to persuade her too. Anyway, the point is...

Always Lead With Emotional Copy In Nutritional Supplement Ads.

Okay, onward.

What emotions should you appeal to in your copy?

Here are seven to start you off:

1. Fear

2. Greed

3. Vanity

4. Lust

5. Pride

6. Envy

7. Laziness

Of course, the more emotions you appeal to in your promotion, the more people you will reach... and the deeper you will reach them.

In supplement controls, though, the most common emotion is fear. Health consumers are afraid of suffering pain, disease, illness, and death. They might be afraid of wasting their money or time on another supplement. And they may be afraid of going to a nursing home or being dependent on their children or grandchildren.

The second most common emotion in supplement copy is greed; the desire to have it all in life. Health consumers want more energy for new adventures. They might want their mobility back so they can continue going on holiday.

And the third most powerful emotion in supplement advertising is hope; the promise of a better life.

In fact, the best supplement controls start by appealing to fear and greed, then quickly transition to hope. Here's an example from the Health Sciences Institute which gives the reader hope of a better life:

"You may no longer have to fear these dreaded diseases. And neither do your loved ones. You can give the life-saving information we uncover to your children and grandchildren—and ensure that your loved ones prosper in the years to come!"

You know, emotion is so pivotal to the success of supplement advertising that, if your copy is generally good... but not selling... it is usually for one of three reasons:

1. The copy is not emotional enough

2. The copy is emotional but insincere

3. The copy plays on the wrong emotion.

So, if you have an ad or sales letter that isn't performing and you can't work out why, this is a good place to start. Try to identify the emotions you are targeting. Is the lead emotional enough? Does it sound sincere? WHAT emotions does the lead appeal to? Are they emotions your market can resonate with?

If you don't know the answer to these questions, then it usually helps to go back to your research. Best way to determine the emotions your market experience? Talk to people one-on-one, ask lots of questions, and listen. The moment you can sense the emotion in their voice, dig deeper, and ask more questions on that subject.

Finally, here's a good test you can apply to your copy immediately, courtesy of the great Clayton Makepeace. He calls it "the forehead slap" test, and it's simple to apply:

Review your copy and ask, "would my prospect wake up in the middle of the night, slap their forehead, and think 'oh no!'"?

Example: "*Flush Deadly Toxins Out Of Your Body*".

Now, nobody would wake up and say, "Oh no, I forgot to flush the deadly toxins out of my colon!"

If the message behind your copy is not something that would make your prospect wake up in the middle of the night and slap their forehead, then it's probably not relatable and emotional enough.

The Most Powerful Word In Advertising

Can you guess what it is?

It's not "free".

It's ...

YOU.

The late great Eugene Schwartz, author of Breakthrough Advertising and a prolific copywriter, said in a seminar that, if an ad didn't have the word "you" in it 100 times, then he didn't like it very much. Why?

It's simple, really. It's because buyers care little of what interests you and what you want...

They Want Service For Themselves!

And it's usually the case that your own interests are not the same as your customers'. So, if the customer smells even a whiff of stinky self-interest from the advertiser, it immediately repels them.

And, countless sales tests have proven that the appeals you like the best will rarely sell the best. How come?

Well, Claude Hopkins reasoned that nobody knows enough people to average up their desires to represent the whole market.

So, even if you are in your market, your own desires are very unlikely to reflect the desires of the many.

Case in point: John Hopkins Medicine published a highly-successful, long-running control which contains the word "you" 58 times in a 6-page letter.

Anyway… let's get down to brass tacks. How can you use this mighty powerful word to your advantage? Well, the answer isn't very sexy (but is effective) …

Study Your Market To Within An Inch Of Your Life!

Gather as much material as you can get your greedy little hands on… talk to people directly… and study ads that have and haven't worked.

When you've got the materials laid out on your desk, and you understand your customer better than your own family, what next?

You Write An Ad That Blows Their Socks Off!

An ad that speaks to the desires of your prospect. And ad that focusses entirely on the reader. And that offers great service.

Okay, I realize I left out a few details there—it's clearly not as simple as doing research then just banging out a winning ad.

For now, I just want to impart that you can only write a good advertisement if you first understand the person you are talking to better than they know themselves.

More:

When it comes to crafting the ad, your research only pays off if you write as though you are talking to the person holding the piece of paper in their hand or reading your sales letter on their computer… and nobody else.

Nobody else in the world exists.

It doesn't matter what your boss, or your mother, or your husband or wife think of your advertisement. It's not for them. You are speaking only to an individual in your market.

You know what causes them pain when they wake up in the morning… and you are their knight in shining armor swooping in to save them.

Not I, I, I…

YOU, YOU, YOU!

PART II:

PREPARING YOUR AD

Do This Before You Write A Word Of Copy

Righty-o, let's chat some more about this research malarkey.

But before we do, if you're thinking… "Yeah, yeah. I get it. Research is important. Can we move on to the juicy stuff?" … then please just put the book down—you've already lost.

I know because my reaction was the same for a long time.

I kept reading about research being the foundation of great marketing. I understood the importance of research *intellectually*, but I didn't execute.

Perhaps because research is difficult (thinking is hard work, isn't it?). Possibly because it seems boring. I don't know. Anyway, it was only when I started APPLYING the information that follows that I truly understood its importance.

And, once it finally sunk in and I started giving deep research a serious chunk of time in projects, it coincided with a dramatic increase in the ease and effectiveness of my writing.

And, if you are responsible for writing direct response copy (or want to be), then research isn't just important, it's absolutely critical. In other words:

You Cannot Write A Winning Promotion Without First Doing A Lot Of Research!

Proof?

The late great copywriter Eugene Schwartz—who beat the control a whopping 85% of the time for the biggest mailers in the world—would read the manuscript of each book his ads were to sell, at least 7 times.

Clayton Makepeace, the world's highest-paid copywriter, whose promotions have generated over $1.5 billion in sales, says on his blog:

"The success of your direct mail piece, print ad, or online sales page is determined to a tremendous extent by the quality of the research you do before you write a single word".

And David Ogilvy, advertising pioneer, copywriter, and founder of the world-famous agency Ogilvy & Mather, dedicated an entire chapter in his book Ogilvy on Advertising to research. He called it "18 Miracles of Research", and the chapter kicks off:

"Advertising people who ignore research are as dangerous as generals who ignore decodes of enemy signals."

Are you persuaded? Okay then, let's get down to business. Here is how to do research for a direct response promotion which, of course, includes nutritional supplements and other health products.

First, dart around and gather as much information as you can. Specifically:

1. On your market…

2. On your prospective customer…

3. And on your product

If you are a copywriter, ask your client for copies of current and past controls, ads and letters that haven't worked in the past, all product sales materials, any information they have on their competitors—their products, marketing, ads, etc. The more, the better.

If you're a marketing director, president or owner of a health company, or if you are involved in the process of marketing nutritional supplements in any other capacity, then you may not have the information you need.

If that's the case, you'll need to go hunting like a squirrel after nuts. Get everything ever printed on the subject; every review or comment from consumers you can get your hands on; the total consumer spend on your product type each year; the total amount spent by the market each year; the percentage of readers to which your product appeals.

You get the idea.

Then, once you have all this information, scoop it up into your greedy little squirrel paws like you've

just found a lifetime's supply of macadamia nuts…
and… dump it all on your desk.

Speaking of squirrels, did you know that, despite
spending the majority of their life hunting, they reject
pretty much every nut they find? The reason, I
understand, is that the very light nuts have probably
been hollowed.

Similarly, you as a copywriter are only interested in
the hot and steamy nuggets in that pile of information
on your desk. Most of it will be scrapped and not used
in your ad. But here's the kicker…

Just like a squirrel, you first have to seek the
information and go through it before you know
whether it's good enough to use. If you don't gather
your materials first, then you won't even have the
opportunity to gather all the relevant facts.

Finally, here's the step most marketers and
copywriters will never take (that's also the most
important) …

Talk To Real People In Your Market.

Talk to them about the problems your product
solves. Ask questions… and listen. For example, if
you sell a supplement that reduces arthritis-associated
joint pain, find people with arthritis and ask how it
affects them. Does it hurt during the night and affect
their sleep? What has been the biggest change in their
lifestyle since they started getting arthritis symptoms?
You get the idea.

Another great source of information if you are selling nutritional supplements is the doctor or expert associated with the product. They know it better than anyone else, so take the opportunity to ask them questions.

Okay, what next? What do you do with all this information? What are you looking for?

Ultimately, you need to get in touch with your prospect's deepest desires. What are they already buying and why? What do they fear? What advertising appeals have they responded to in the past? What appeals didn't work? What does the product you are selling do better than any others? What benefits does it provide the customer?

For every project, I have a list of 76 questions I find the answers to before writing a word of copy. Some of the answers come from literature, some from the client, some from past promotions, and some from direct conversation with people in the market. To give you an idea of the questions you can ask, here's a small selection from my own list:

1. What are your prospects afraid of?

2. What causes them pain?

3. What keeps them awake at night?

4. What do they desire?

5. What do they want more than anything?

6. What are their values like?

7. Why do they need what you are selling?

8. How aware are they of the problem your product solves, on a scale of 1-10?

Why Copy Is The Least Important Factor In A Direct Marketing Promotion

Gary Halbert, one of the greatest marketing minds of our time, once published a newsletter about when he used to teach advertising at his local community college. The Prince of Print would ask each of his students:

"If you and I both owned a hamburger stand and we were in a contest to see who could sell the most hamburgers, what advantages would you most like to have on your side to help you win?"

Some of the students said they would choose superior meat from which to make their burgers. Others wanted sesame seed buns. Others wanted a prime location. Someone usually wanted to be able to offer the lowest prices. And so on. After the students finished telling him what advantages they would like, Halbert would say:

"O.K., I'll give you every single advantage you have asked for. I only want one advantage and, if you will give it to me, I will (when it comes to selling burgers) whip the pants off all of you!"

"What advantage do you want?" they would ask.

"The only advantage I want," Halbert replied...

"Is A Starving Crowd!"

Halbert was demonstrating that the single most important success factor in direct marketing is a group of people who are *starving for a solution.*

And, it reminds me of an old formula which explains the importance of the different elements of a direct response marketing campaign. The numbers aren't exact—testing before the internet was very slow and expensive—but it goes something like this:

70% of the success of a direct marketing promotion is determined by your list…

… 20% by the offer…

… and 10% by the copy.

Like the Starving Crowd story, this formula demonstrates that copy is important… but it's not the critical factor. Actually, it is relatively unimportant. Here's what I mean.

Smoking hot copy with an irresistible offer, sent to a crappy list, won't generate sales….

But a mediocre offer explained with shoddy copy, sent to a super-hot list can still line your pockets with cold hard cash.

Does this still apply if you're not using a mailing list?

Yes, absolutely. If you're not using mailing lists, how *are* you finding your customers?

Do you use Google Ads to direct prospects to your opt-in or sales page? Do you run full-page magazine advertorials? If you target the wrong keywords or use the wrong magazines... It really doesn't matter how strong your offer or copy is.

If your offer isn't presented to a group of people who are starving for your solution... then you won't generate many sales.

You know, this idea of feeding a starving crowd goes beyond the list of people you are selling to. It also applies to your market as a whole. A market is just a group of people with a problem or desire. If your market isn't hungry, and if they don't have the means to pay for a solution, then you've already lost.

The market comes first...

Then the product or service...

Then the offer... ...

Then the copy.

Essentially, the closer your product comes to fulfilling what your prospects are hungry for... the better your marketing results will be.

Have you noticed that this book isn't just about *writing*? Now you know why.

How To Craft An Irresistible Supplement Offer

Assuming you are already selling a product, the next most important element in your marketing promotions (and THE most important element of your sales message) is your offer.

Why?

Because strong copy will NOT overcome a weak offer (for example, a low-quality supplement being sold at a premium and without a guarantee) …

But a strong offer will often succeed in spite of weak copy!

Now, I don't mean a special offer like a discount on your normal price. Instead, think of an offer like a business proposition. The most common offer is something like:

"If you give me X amount of money, I will give you X product or service in return."

That's where most advertiser's stop. But the offer can be made a LOT juicier. For example, as a copywriter you might make the following standard offer:

"Give me £5000 and I will write a sales letter for you."

Put yourself in the shoes of a client. Is that an attractive offer?

Hmm, I'm not sure. What if you don't deliver on time? What if you just swipe another ad, practically word-for-word? What if you take the money and run?

No. How about this instead:

"I will write a sales letter for you. Don't pay me anything upfront, just 5% of gross profit from the campaign. I'll have it on your desk in two weeks. And, if I don't, you can deduct 0.5% from my fee for each day it's late. "

If you're a copywriter, I'm not saying you *should* make an offer like that. It doesn't always make sense —for you or the client. But, can you see how powerful it would be in some situations?

More:

If you are selling nutritional supplements, a basic offer might be:

"If you give me X amount of money, I will send you one month's supply of X supplement."

Or you could sweeten the deal:

"We'll send you one month's supply of X supplement. Try it for the whole month without cost or obligation. We'll even pay for the shipping and handling. If you notice an improvement in your arthritis symptoms and want to continue taking the supplement, then just send us a check. If not, or if you would like to stop taking X supplement for any other reason, then you don't pay a penny."

Many marketer's and business owners squirm at the thought of making an irresistible offer.

"Won't my return's sky-rocket?"

"How can I expect to make any money with an offer like that?"

"Doesn't this de-value my product?"

No, no, and no.

If your offer includes a guarantee, for example, you might be tempted to keep the time-frame short (like a 30-day money back guarantee). But that would be a mistake because, counter-intuitively, the longer your guarantee, the lower your returns.

I don't know why. Perhaps customers just forget about the guarantee. It doesn't really matter why, anyway. The point is: if you increase the length of the guarantee, you will normally increase sales and decrease returns.

Truth is, a good offer isn't one that mindlessly slashes the price of the product to make more sales. An effective offer delivers great service to your customer's. It reduces their risk. It helps them overcome their doubts. And, it allows them to trial your product and see the results for themselves without risk.

In fact, it is my contention that it is your moral obligation to do everything in your power to help your customer's access your product. If it's a good product (and you DO have a good product, right?) then you can only solve their problem if they buy it.

What this all boils down to is…

If you want to write an ad that sells your product… that beats the existing control… then you MUST spend time and effort looking for ways to sweeten your offer.

Pricing Hacks To Increase Profits

Now, I don't know what type of supplement you sell, so let's imagine you have a product which helps relieve the symptoms of arthritis.

I estimate that, as a healthcare professional, I helped diagnose over 6,600 men and women, many of whom suffered from osteoarthritis.

When I first met them, they were very vulnerable and often opened up about their feelings and worries. The women were typically frustrated about not being able to do the things they enjoyed, like gardening, knitting and cooking. They hated relying on their family members to do simple tasks they could previously do independently. They despised their appearances, like gnarled hands and knobbly knees.

Men, on the other hand, hated needing someone's help, typically their wife's help, in doing ordinary man things like buttoning a shirt or using cufflinks… or… being embarrassed in front of others when unable to perform basic man duties, like twisting open a stubborn jar lid. Unlike women, it wasn't not being able to do something that frustrated them, but the fact they needed help.

In extreme cases, the pain and debilitation of arthritis becomes so overwhelming and consistent that they stop going to church or socializing with their friends. As a result, they felt lonely and isolated. So, the question is:

How Much Is Your Supplement Worth To Somebody Like This?

How much do you think they would pay for a return to independence and the ability to do their gardening again?

Here's the point: if you are selling a good supplement to a hungry market, it's probably worth a lot more than you think!

Therefore, you might well be undercharging.

The solution? Test different prices.

Okay, on to the juicy stuff. Here is a checklist of proven pricing tactics you can use to boost profits:

1. **Add special reports, interview transcripts, books and CDs**. This will increase the perceived value of your offer, which means you can increase your price and average order value. A supplement which sells for $29 could easily sell for $59 or more with valuable information attached.

2. **Price at "a penny less"**. Ever wondered why products are sold for "a penny less" (e.g. for $19.99 rather than $20)? It's because the human mind always rounds to the lowest number. A prospect may not be comfortable spending $20, but under $20 is fine…

even if there's only a penny difference. So, only announce the price of shipping and handling AFTER your prospect has made the decision to buy. This should ideally be in another place entirely—online, on the order page; offline, on the order device.

3. **Trivialize the price**. In your copy, present the price and then trivialize it. For example: "That's less than a penny a day."

4. **Compare to individual nutrients**. Compare the price of your product to the price of buying each nutrient in the supplement separately.

5. **Compare to healthcare**. Compare the price to the cost of surgery, doctor visits, prescription drugs, etc.

6. **Compare to a commodity**. Compare the price to that of a mundane item or commodity, like a cup of coffee or a gallon of gas.

7. **Present offers at different prices**. For example, "BEST DEAL: 4 bottles for $150 + free shipping; BETTER DEAL: 2 bottles for $100; GREAT DEAL: 1 bottle for $60.

8. **Test prices ending in 7**. The legendary marketer and copywriter Ted Nicholas found through significant testing that prices ending in the number 7 work better than any other number, e.g. $19.97.

The Case Against Discounting

When Howard Wein moved to Philadelphia in 2004 to open a boutique steakhouse called Barclay Prime, he knew he needed to offer more than good food. Why?

Because over 25% of restaurants fail within 12 months; 60% in the first three years.

Restaurants fail for a number of reasons. Expenses are high. There's an army of competitors. And, it's tough to convince people it's a great place to eat. Wein's solution?

A $120 Cheesesteak!

Yes, really. He took the steak sandwich to a new level—we're talking wagyu beef, truffles, truffle cheese, truffle butter and foie gras—then added a premium price tag. And it got people talking.

In fact, the cheesesteak generated so much buzz it was featured on USA Today and The Wall Street Journal. David Beckham ate one. Barclay Prime's executive chef was asked to cook one on The Late Show for more than 3 million viewers. Of course, the sandwich wasn't just a showpiece for Barclay Prime.

Against the odds, it helped the restaurant thrive. And what the Barclay Prime Cheesesteak demonstrates is that...

You Don't Have To Slash The Price Of Your Product In Order To Sell It!

In fact, you should consider doing the exact opposite. Here's why: it's usually easier to convince someone to spend $300 than $30.

People will buy a $50k car with barely a thought, then drive 30 miles out their way to get a 2-cent discount on a gallon of gas. Mental... but true.

The $120 cheesesteak also shows that people judge a product largely on its price. Why? Probably because they are not the subject experts. So, they assume, rightly or wrongly, that the higher priced option is better. It's an easy method for a consumer to select the best product.

In other words, a product which costs more than average is considered to be above average. And, a product which costs less than average is considered less than average.

You know, the obvious conclusion to draw from this information is that you should test a higher price than you are currently charging.

But it's also a strong case against discounting. Here's why in the words of the late great Claude Hopkins:

"Before a prospect is converted, it is approximately as hard to get half price for your product as it is to get the full price for it."

So why, then, is discounting so commonplace? Honestly, I don't know. But I reason that cheapness (in the form of a discount) is appealing. Obviously, we want to buy things for the lowest price possible. Therefore, an appeal of cheapness can be effective for selling products.

And, discounting has its place.

In his superb book *Read, Fire, Aim*, serial entrepreneur Mark Ford recommends discounting as a strategy to bring in lots of new customers at once for a small business. However, he then goes on to explain that discounting is generally a challenging and problematic way to grow a business.

"Most products…" he explained "… should be sold by emphasizing their qualities and benefits."

The reason why is that, although cheapness *is* appealing, it's not a *strong* appeal. Plus, your market will come to believe that your product is low in price, and therefore low in quality. They will then only be prepared to pay your discounted price. Here are some better advertising appeals for the health market:

- Greater strength

- Vigor

- Endurance

- The possibility of a longer life

- Greater ability to travel, enjoy hobbies, etc.

- More independence

Get the idea?

How To Find The Optimal Selling Price For Your Supplement

In the aforementioned *Ready, Fire, Aim*, Mark Ford proposes four stages of business growth.

Stage 1: zero to £1 million in revenue.

Stage 2: $1 million to $10 million in revenue.

Stage 3: $10 million to $50 million in revenue.

Stage 4: $50 to $100 million plus in revenue.

Ford contends that the problems, challenges and opportunities are different in each stage of entrepreneurial growth.

Take stage 1, for example:

"Main problem: don't really know what you are doing

"Main challenge: making the first profitable sale

"Main opportunity: increasing cash flow and becoming profitable

"Main skill needed: selling the product"

Selling the product. That's what we are concerned with here. And, of course, when you sell a product, the question inevitably comes: How much should it cost?

Well, you might recall that the price of your product is part of your offer. Remember, a basic offer (or business proposition) looks like this:

"If you give me X amount of money, I will give you X product in return."

If you have not yet sold your product then you are faced with the question above, and the price of your product has a major impact on your sales, secondary only to your market (or the media you use) and the appeal of the product itself. So how much should you charge?

The answer isn't very sexy. It certainly won't inspire you. But the answer IS straightforward:

Charge What Everyone Else Is Charging!

You know, I was once contacted out of the blue by an old neighbor. She had heard I was running my own marketing business and wanted some free advice on a venture she was trying to start with her partner.

Side note: I learned early on that people only act on what they pay for; when they've got some skin in the game. So, please do not contact me for free advice. However, if you are hungry for more information… or… if you would like to discuss the possibility of working with me, then you can find the relevant details at the end of this book.

Anyway…

It turned out my old neighbor had just been made redundant. Her partner was a real estate agent who wanted out. And, they'd been on a European classic car tour together had the time of their lives. However, it also cost a fortune, and the service they received in return for their hard-earned cash was poor. Ever since they had dreamt of starting their own classic car company.

Being paid to drive around the south of France in a classic car sounds pretty good, doesn't it?

So, there we were, sat at their kitchen table. The walls and floors were stripped back to stone (they'd been in the middle of a renovation when she was made redundant).

The entrepreneurs showed me the website they'd created. They explained how they'd spent around $500 on Facebook Ads, and all they got in return were some "likes" on their post from people who clearly weren't interested in classic car tours.

They had no money left in the bank but, they were willing to take out a loan if I advised them to spend more on advertising.

My heart sank.

They were clearly desperate to make this thing work. And I knew how it felt. I'd been there when I left my healthcare career behind. I was like a worm trying to climb a mountain.

Anywho.

After some discussion, they sat back and asked: "What do we need to do?"

Whoosh. What a big question that was. They were effectively asking me, who three years prior knew nothing of business or marketing (and who still has a hell of a lot to learn), how to get a classic car company off the ground with as little cost as possible… and… without plunging them into debt.

Frankly, it scared the pants off me they were willing to go into debt based on my advice!

Luckily for them, I had a good answer. An answer I was confident they wouldn't get from any marketing agency in a 100-mile radius.

I knew they wanted to hear that I had some fancy trick up my sleeve. That if they just followed this secret Facebook advertising hack, they would get swamped with bookings. Which is why I could tell they were disappointed when I told them:

"Do What Everyone Else Is Doing"

I suggested they not spend any more money on advertising (they didn't know how). Instead, if they wanted to know the best way to go from zero to "in business", I advised them to look to similar companies who had already managed to do it.

Those companies had done the expensive, time-consuming, and knuckle-grinding work involved in figuring out what works for their market. Nothing I could offer them could come close.

So, I suggested they identify their top five future competitors and call them up. Ask for the names of the people in charge of their marketing. "Tell them you are a marketing student", I said, "because you are." And ask for a 15-minute informational interview.

You know, I could tell they really didn't want to hear this. And you probably you don't want to hear that the same applies to find the optimum selling price for a new product.

Am I right? I don't know. But it is what I would do if I were you. And I learned this approach from Mark Ford, who has built several multi-million-dollar businesses in different industries. So, I think you're in good hands.

Onward.

Okay, so what if you are already selling a product?

If that's the case then you have, of course, already established a price for it. Does that mean you should leave the price as it is? Maybe. If you have tested different prices and you are currently charging at the most profitable level, then yes, it sounds like you've found your optimum selling price. (And you probably didn't need to read this chapter, so thanks for persisting). However...

If you've been selling your product for a consistent, arbitrary price... you might be surprised at how much more crisp ones you could put in your pocket simply by TESTING!

Run split tests. Try different prices and measure which is most profitable. Ideally, track the lifetime value of the customer's you get at each sale price. It might be that you make a smaller profit on the front end with a lower price, but because you get more customer's, you make more on the backend in repeat sales.

How To Develop A White-Hot Unique Selling Proposition

Ever seen the New Zealand rugby team—the All Blacks—perform The Haka?

At the start of every game, they stand facing the opposition on the half-way line and perform a battle preparation dance once used by Maori warriors. And, quite frankly…

It's Terrifying!

It has always amazed me how opposition team are forced to stand and watch. You can see the fear in their eyes. Even watching The Haka on TV makes the hairs on the back of my neck stand on end.

I can't believe that any man could stand and watch their opponent perform The Haka immediately before going to "war" … and not be affected by it.

It's the All Blacks' secret weapon.

And, whilst it would be unfair to attribute their success to The Haka, the fact remains that they are the most successful men's rugby union team ever.

Since their international debut in 1903, they've lost to only 6 of the 19 nations they've played against in test matches. And, since the introduction of the world rugby rankings in 2003, they have held the number one spot longer than all the other teams combined.

Anyway, when I was watching the All Black's perform The Haka in a recent documentary, it got me to wondering...

If The Haka is so powerful, why is New Zealand the only team to use it?

And the answer is simple: it's a traditional dance which is unique to New Zealand. No other team could use it, even if they wanted to. And you know what?

The Haka is like New Zealand's Unique Selling Proposition (USP).

It's what separates them from every other team in the world. It's their competitive advantage.

Now, The Haka sells the opposition on the idea that the All Blacks can't be beaten.

In marketing, a USP is used for a different purpose. It's basically your answer to the question:

"Why Should I Deal With You, Not The Other Guy?"

Most businesses will say they have a USP, but it often provides no tangible benefit to their clients, such that it really doesn't distinguish them from their competitors at all.

In fact, if they told a prospective customer their USP, they would probably think: "so what?"

Not ideal.

Instead, a USP should elevate your product or organization to a position of notable superiority over your competition. And to do that, you must offer your prospect or client a unique and distinctive benefit or advantage which is beyond that of your competitors.

For example, when Domino's first entered the home-delivered pizza market, they said…

"Hot, juicy, delicious pizza—delivered to your door in thirty minutes or less—or it's yours absolutely free."

When they first started, no other company would guarantee hot pizza delivery in half an hour. The USP was therefore so distinctive that Domino's virtually owned the market for several years.

Let's break it down and analyze what made their USP such a success.

First, it provided multiple benefits their customers wanted:

• Hot, juicy, delicious pizza

• Delivered to their door

• Delivered in 30 minutes or less

Not only that, each one of these benefits was tangible, specific, and measurable. Therefore, the claim was easy to believe, which made it easy to buy.

Second, Domino's guaranteed the delivery (pardon the pun) of those benefits. If your pizza wasn't hot, delicious and delivered in 30 minutes or less, it was yours at no cost.

That's Ballsy!

There really was no risk for the customer. If they ordered from another pizza delivery company (if they could find one), it would probably take longer than 30 minutes and/or arrive cold. So, what did they have to lose by ordering from Dominos?

Third, very few companies at the time delivered pizza at all. And no other company was guaranteeing to deliver pizza in 30 minutes or less. The proposition truly was unique in the pizza delivery market.

So, there you have it. A USP should be:

1. A benefit that your market wants

2. A benefit or advantage that none of your competitor's offer

3. Specific and measurable—e.g. 24/7 service, 365 days/year; Lifetime guarantee; Contracted by the FBI

Here's how to find your USP: research your market, then find and focus on the one niche, need or gap that is most sorely lacking.

Here are some ways you might be able to set your supplement product apart from the competition:

Unique recipe

Does your product have more of a certain ingredient, making it more effective? Is there a unique combination of ingredients?

New ingredient

Did you discover a "new" ingredient for your supplement that provides some unique benefit? Did you find a new way to use an already well-known ingredient?

Expert or celebrity endorsement

A great way to add individuality to supplement ads is to sell on behalf of a doctor—someone who takes pride in their accomplishments and recommendations. This has the added bonus of providing proof and credibility. Is there anybody in your company or associated with your product who you could sell on behalf of?

Better absorption

"Expensive pee" is a real and widespread objection to supplement usage. And, for some supplements, our bodies can't absorb the ingredients, which might reduce the effect. Have you found a way to help the body absorb your supplement better than competing products?

Pill-free

Some prospects might avoid buying your product if it means taking another pill. So, if you've developed a product which enables consumers to take fewer (or no) pills, then that's a strong benefit. Alternatively, if it is a pill, does it have a pleasant flavor? Is it enclosed in vegetarian or vegan gel capsules?

Side-effect-free

Note the side effects people experience from prescription drugs and how your product can relieve them. Or, position your product as a side-effect-free alternative to a prescription drug.

Safety

Consumers are concerned about the safety and purity of ingredients. You can ease their fears by explaining that your ingredients are pre-tested to verify their potency and purity. Tell the story of how the product is tested. Does your product adhere to the FDA's Good Manufacturing Process (GMP)? Are your ingredients organic?

Source of ingredients

You could distinguish yourself not only by citing the quality of ingredients, and their safety/potency, but also their source.

Is the location of growth pollution-free?

Are your farming practices ecological?

Mentioning the source of an ingredient paints a picture in the mind of prospects, and vision drives decision.

What benefit does the location bring the consumer? Perhaps it was harvested in South Africa, which means it was carefully controlled by South African conservation organizations.

Chemical free

Consumers are looking for natural alternatives to a high-tech lifestyle. They feel more comfortable buying foods and supplements with fewer chemical components.

Ascent Protein is a great example of this. Their protein supplements contain only very recognizable natural ingredients, which gives you more confidence you are buying a safe and healthy product.

World impact

More and more consumers are interested in the larger impact of their purchase on the world. Does your company invest in better education programs for families who harvest green tea in India? Does it donate a portion of its profits to charity?

Customization

An emerging group of people is looking for products they can customize to their needs. The field of nutrigenomics is emerging, so this market is likely to grow.

Could you use a detailed questionnaire to find the right supplement for each person?

Do you use genetic mapping to personalize formulas for customers?

Okay, onward.

So which USP is best?

There are so many ways to position your product uniquely that it begs the question, which is best?

The answer depends on your market. Do some research. Look at the ads of your competitors and figure out what their USP is. Speak to people in your market and find out what they really want.

Some markets, for example, might want a supplement with all-natural ingredients, whereas others might be more interested in customizing the product to meet their needs.

And, remember that this is called a unique selling proposition for a reason. To be unique, it must be something none of your competitors are offering. To sell, it must be a benefit your market wants. And to be a strong proposition, it must be offer something tangible and specific.

How To Sweep Aside Scepticism

If you want to write great nutritional supplement copy, the next few pages might be the most important information you will ever read.

Allow me to prove it to you.

In the early 19th century, passenger elevators had been installed in England and America, but the hemp ropes that held the elevators up would often break and kill passengers.

Then one day, a man by the name of Elisha Otis invented a device that could prevent an elevator from falling when its rope broke.

But he had a problem.

In 1853, Otis sold only three elevators. In the first few months of 1854, he sold none. Seemingly, everybody was too scared of elevators to take a chance on his invention.

So, the entrepreneur set up a dramatic demonstration at the Worlds Fair in New York's Crystal Palace.

Here's how the Otis Elevator Company, still going strong today, recall the event:

"Perched on a hoisting platform high above the crowd at New York's Crystal Palace, a pragmatic mechanic shocked the crowd when he dramatically cut the only rope suspending the platform on which he was standing. The platform dropped a few inches, but then came to a stop. His revolutionary new safety brake had worked, stopping the platform from crashing to the ground. "All safe, gentlemen!" the man proclaimed."

After that, Otis ended 1854 with seven sales, and the following year he sold 15. But that was only the beginning of his company's success.

By 1873 there were 2,000 Otis elevators in use, and they later fitted elevators in the Eiffel Tower, the Empire State Building, and the World Trade Center.

It wouldn't be an exaggeration to say that Otis's invention transformed the way we live. Real estate investors could now build high without buying more land. High-rise living quarters went from being the cheapest to the most expensive. And the turning point was… without a doubt…

The Dramatic Demonstration!

You see, when Otis invented his safety device, the public was very skeptical of elevators. I guess they weren't particularly keen on falling to their death from a great height.

Selling using normal methods was unsuccessful. Perhaps the buyers didn't believe that the invention really was safe and trustworthy. The risk was too high. The demonstration solved that problem.

Simply, Otis put his life on the line to <u>prove</u> his invention was safe.

In advertising, just like when Otis tried to tell people he had found a way to make elevators safe, each claim is met with a corresponding level of resistance. You must prove and credentialize your claims.

Gary Bencivenga, the greatest living copywriter, says:

"When you make your credibility an essential, highly visible part of your marketing, persuasion can flow like silk because your most commonly encountered enemy—skepticism—is largely swept aside. — Bencivenga Bullets, Bullet #29: The Secret of How to Sell Anything

In his book No B.S. Sales Success in The New Economy, Dan Kennedy says:

"Having a preponderance of proof make it possible to sell with 100% effectiveness, 100% of the time. If you want to win with every presentation of every proposition, make sure you have an overwhelming amount of proof that what you are selling is a great deal, have an overwhelming quality of proof and have proof that is influential."

Okay, so how can you apply this?

Well, you can use demonstration in your ads. Eugene Schwartz was brilliant at this. Here's one of his headlines:

"IF YOU'RE OVER THIRTY—THIS IS THE BEST EXERCISE YOU CAN DO FOR YOUR FACE, YOUR BODY AND YOUR HEART!"

The entire ad was a demonstration of what the book would do for the reader if they ordered. The body copy took the reader through the three steps they needed to follow to increase their energy levels.

How can you use this in supplement copy?

Here's one example. If you are selling a supplement that helps improve vision, say:

"Do this eye test now. Mark your score down. Try the product for 3 months then retake the test. If your score isn't any higher then we'll give you a refund."

As you can see, demonstration is a very powerful form of proof. Perhaps the most powerful. But there are many others, too. Testimonials, for example. That's the next section. Before we get to that, here are some other ways to prove your claims.

Write in the voice of an expert

This is a classic approach to nutritional supplement advertising. The health market is very sophisticated. They've seen a lot of ads; as much as 2-3 a week. To make it worse, the media tend to discredit supplements, and doctors distrust them. People are very, very skeptical. Their gut reaction to an ad is:

"Who the hell are you and why should I listen to you?".

Still, there are a lot of people who need solutions to their health problems. You just have to work hard to build trust and persuade them you can help. You have to prove it.

One way to do this is to write in the voice of an expert; typically, a doctor. Hearing from a doctor gives the reader hope. Doctors are seen as "insiders" with knowledge the rest of us couldn't possibly possess. They are trusted immediately.

Expert lift note

If for some reason the doctor or expert behind your product does not want the ad to appear as though written by them, you could feature their words on a lift note, or as a testimonial.

Profile your expert in a sidebar

Another approach to leveraging the credibility of an expert is to feature them in a sidebar. You should dedicate plenty of space to their credentials and also weave them into your main copy.

Quote a recognized expert

If you don't have a medical expert on board, pull in quotes from a published book from a recognized expert. Dr. Stephen Sinatra or Dr. Christine Northrup, for example. Of course, get written permission to refer to their published material in your copy.

Sell to the doctor

More and more people are consulting their doctor about taking supplements. Provide adequate evidence from sources that will stand on their own against their doctor's advice. Include citations of specific studies. Possibly include a lift note they can take to the doctor. Highlight how difficult it is for physicians to keep up with the volume of nutritional research—and how you will provide the pertinent information.

Guarantee

Providing a guarantee is a strong advantage of natural over pharmaceutical.

Can you imagine paying for a prescription and then asking for a refund if it didn't work? It just wouldn't wash. Use this to your advantage.

It can be as simple as saying, in effect: "If this doesn't work, it costs you nothing. If it does, it will change your life."

Use social proof

You know Jeff Walker, the internet marketer behind the *Product Launch Formula*? His method has helped countless marketers create multi-million dollar launches and a big part of the reason why is that the formula leverages social proof.

You can use this in supplement advertising, too.

Although most people get supplement recommendations from doctors and print (books, magazines, etc.), they also ask their friends and family.

They want social proof.

People want to see that your product changed somebody's life in the way they want to change theirs. You can achieve this by using powerful case histories and testimonials.

Leverage the press

If your product, type of product or business has been featured in the press... use it! This is possibly better than using a private expert, who could later deny providing an endorsement.

Combine evidence behind each ingredient

A big challenge with supplement advertising is that few products have been scientifically tested with all ingredients together, which makes it hard to back up product claims.

One way to get around this is to find evidence for the effect of individual ingredients, then make a case that they could be more reactive together.

Always be specific

Generalities are received with caution. Consumers assume that advertisers exaggerate, but a specific claim is either true or false.

And since nobody expects you to outright lie, the specific claim is believable.

Be very specific about the number of products, the percentage of each ingredient... and... when using scientific evidence, be very specific about which scientists and studies you are referring to.

Be specific about exactly how your supplement helped others. For example,

"24.7 kg weight loss in 21 days" rather than "significant weight loss".

Finally, if you don't have specific facts to prove your claims, consider investing in experiments to gain these facts.

Scientific evidence

I've left this until last, but it's probably the most obvious form of proof in supplement advertising. It's pretty much impossible to write supplement ads without citing scientific evidence, not least because the FTC requires that you back up your claims.

The Power Of Social Proof

Recently, I had the motive to change my accountant.

I had it in my mind to choose a guy I'd met a couple of years earlier. He was a family friend who had been very generous with his time when I was starting out in business. But there were still a few other good options.

I'd met a number of accountants as a Digital Marketing Manager and learned who the good ones were.

Then my wife came back from work one day and said that her colleague's brother used to work for the same firm as the accountant I had in mind.

In fact, they had referred to him as a "super accountant". Apparently, he was qualified in multiple areas of accountancy; an uncommon trait.

A few days later, I decided to get my ass in gear and finally make the switch.

And guess what? I chose the super accountant!

Yet, it was only on reflection that I realized I'd been influenced by this third-hand comment. It tipped my decision over the edge.

That, My Friend, Is The Power Of Social Proof!

If you try to tell the reader how great you are, how you achieved this or that, how you helped such and such a client, they just won't believe you (or won't care). It comes across as bragging. It is much, much more effective to let other people do the bragging for you.

In his book, No B.S. Sales Success in The New Economy, the legendary Dan Kennedy wrote:

"If you under-utilize testimonials, there you are, huffing, puffing, straining, and struggling to convey your marketing message and convince of your virtues, while you keep an entire army of more persuasive, more instantly believable salespeople eager to do the heavy lifting for you free, bound and gagged, locked in the closet, out of sight."

Here's a crash course in collecting and using effective testimonials in your ads and marketing materials:

1. If you are a copywriter, don't start writing an ad for a client until you've got a handful of testimonials available

2. If you sell nutritional supplements and no-one is volunteering testimonials, then send a short letter with the product to every new customer asking them to scribble down their comments and return in a pre-paid envelope

3. If you are in a position where you can speak to a customer directly about their experience using your

product, then ask them lots of questions. It's hard for people to give you a testimonial off the bat without guidance because they don't know what you are looking for.

Then, condense their answers into one or two sentences that capture the essence of what they're trying to say. And of course, ask them for permission to use whatever you come up with

4. Once you have plenty of testimonials to choose from, try to find one for each major benefit of your product

5. Keep the testimonials short, punchy and powerful—one or two sentences should do it

6. Don't be tempted to remove their objections. Keep them in and show the reader how they were overcome. This helps them get past the objection in their own mind

7. When presenting the testimonial, use as much of the person's name and location as possible

8. If you are using direct mail, consider using one or two testimonials on a lift note... and use one on the order form as a final reminder of how your product will benefit them

The George Costanza School Of Nutritional Supplement Copywriting

Every product and service in the world has flaws. I know it. You know it. Everybody knows it.

So, it's just inevitable that every now and again when writing copy, you will be tempted to embellish the truth.

Surely, if you tell the ugly truth, the reader will throw your ad down in disgust. Won't they?

Actually… no.

Allow me to demonstrate.

There's a great scene in the show, Seinfeld, where George Costanza decides to ignore his gut and do everything in reverse. He walks up to the counter of the diner and introduces himself to a beautiful woman.

"My name is George. I'm unemployed and I live with my parents."

The woman stares at him in disbelief… …

… then leans on the counter, throws back her hair, and gazes lovingly towards George.

"I'm Victoria. Hiiiiii…"

You know, all great comedy is based on reality. So, the next time you are tempted to cover up a flaw, try doing the opposite....

Tell The Truth!

People assume you are going to exaggerate as an advertiser, so astonish them by being totally honest. It's a powerful way to overcome skepticism.

And health markets are more skeptical than most— so honesty is even more important. (It's also the best way to stay on the good side of the FTC... and just the right thing to do all around).

Anyway.

There's a terrific e-book called *Writing Irresistible Copy for Nutritional Supplements*. It's written by Sarah Clachar and features advice from several top-class health copywriters. I highly recommend it.

The reason I bring this up is that the author tackles the issue of dealing with side effects.

Now, it would be easy for an advertiser to brush over side effects. But Carline Cole, the superb and prolific health copywriter, does the opposite.

Cole explains in the book that she was once selling a product that also acted as a powerful blood thinner. So, rather than hide the associated risks, they plastered warnings all over the promotion which said:

"You should not take this if you are already on Coumadin (a pharmaceutical blood thinner)".

According to Cole, the promotion did well despite, or perhaps as a result of, the warning.

Something to think about.

The Truth About Creativity

Have you ever seen Amadeus?

It's a movie about the great composer, Wolfgang Amadeus Mozart.

It won eight Academy Awards, four BAFTA's, four Golden Globes, and a Director's Guild of America (DGA) award.

The movie also reveals that Mozart was… well… a strange character.

Despite being a creative genius, Mozart had a rather infantile sense of humor. The man who was composing from the age of 5… who performed for royalty… and who is widely considered the most gifted classical musician of all time…

Loved A Good Poo Joke!

Yep. Many letters and song lyrics written by Mozart are scattered with toilet humor. My personal favorite is a snippet from a letter Mozart sent to his cousin:

"Oui, by the love of my skin, I shit on your nose, so it runs down your chin…"

Astonishing.

Apparently, when Margaret Thatcher went to see the play of Amadeus, she refused to believe that a man who produced such elegant music could be so foul-mouthed.

So, the Director sent copies of Mozart letters to number ten Downing Street the very next day. But still, such was the contrast between his music and humor, Mrs. Thatcher refused to believe it.

Anyway, I don't just bring up Mozart's unusual character to entertain you. Amadeus reveals another habit of Mozart's that provides tremendous insight into the creative process.

A short scene shows Mozart at a billiards table. Candles burning, he leans over a table scattered with notes. He has a quill, an ink bottle, and a sheet of paper. He takes the yellow billiard ball in his right hand and rolls it.

Bounce... bounce... bounce.

The ball ricochets against the three edges of the table and slowly returns to its original position next to Mozart's sheet of paper.

Each time the ball goes on its journey, Mozart dips his quill in the ink pot and scribbles notes.

Using this technique, Mozart never re-wrote his music; every note remained as it appeared in the first draft.

He had a remarkable ability to tap into his creative power.

A case in point: The night before the famous opera, *Don Giovanni*, Mozart hadn't even begun writing the overture.

According to one account, when Constanze Mozart tried to keep him awake with punch and poetry reading, it had the opposite effect. Mozart went to sleep for a one-hour nap but ended up sleeping through until 5 a.m.

Under massive pressure, Mozart sprang into action, banged out the overture and delivered it to the copyists in two short hours.

So, why did Mozart follow his unusual practice of composing at the billiard's table? Was he just crackers, or is there something more going on?

Well, as Eugene Schwartz explained in one of his seminars, ideas are not created from thin air—like when God created heaven and earth—but rather, through a connection between two or more previously-unconnected facts.

And, it is in the connection of pre-existing facts and ideas that Mozart was so effective.

You see, the mind is a huge network of cells that translates images and thoughts back and forth. When you are focused on a particular task, all of your brain's energy is concentrated on the small number of cells in your conscious mind.

Your conscious mind uses logic, but it doesn't make connections very well. Thus, you cannot produce ideas using your conscious mind alone.

If you want to generate ideas, then you have to get out of the conscious mind. And, that's what Mozart was doing by rolling the billiards ball.

The trajectory of the ball was unpredictable. He had to concentrate and temporarily engage his conscious mind to have the ball arrive back in the same place. By diverting his conscious mind onto something else, his subconscious mind engaged and subsequently spat out notes that Mozart could quickly scribble down.

Okay, so how can you use this to your advantage when writing copy?

Here is one technique:

1. Get yourself a timer. Punch in 33 minutes and 33 seconds. Hit start. And work intensely until the timer buzzes.

2. When the timer buzzes, stop working immediately (even if you're in the middle of a sentence)

3. Punch 5 minutes into the timer, press start, and go do something else. Play with your dog. Make another cup of coffee. Billiards table? Bounce the ball off three sides and try and have it land in the same place.

You must engage your conscious mind on something other than your work. This frees up your subconscious mind to mull over what you've just been concentrating on.

It can make connections and throw new "ideas" (previously unconnected facts) back into your conscious mind when you sit down to work again. As Schwartz explained:

"You've been working, now you create."

Finally, a word of caution: when I first started working this way, I used my iPhone as a timer. And, I quickly noticed that the moment I hit a wall when writing (and sometimes before I'd even got started) my mind drifted.

Like one of Pavlov's dogs with a collar and leash around my neck, I just couldn't resist picking up my phone and mindlessly checking emails or browsing Facebook.

For this technique to work, your conscious mind has to work extremely intensely for the 33 minutes and 33 seconds. So much so that you don't notice time passing and you need the timer to remind you to stop.

For me, having a phone on my desk was a constant distraction. It was far too easy NOT to work intensely.

Perhaps you have a stronger immunity to the addictive powers of smartphones and social media than I do. But, even if that's the case, every morsel of will power you invest in NOT checking your phone while working is energy you could be putting into your copy.

I don't have a mobile phone anymore (a story for another day), but at the time, I got around this problem by turning my phone off and leaving it in another room. I now use a small hand-held timer which cost less than $5 on Amazon.

Anyway.

This is just one way to tap into the power of your creative subconscious every day.

Learn it. Apply it. Profit from it.

And, in the next chapter, I'll show you how to unlock your inner creativity to generate big ideas for kick-ass supplement ads.

A Technique For Producing Breakthrough Ideas

The title of this section is the name of a little-known book by James Webb Young.

Most assume that ideas are spontaneous. That idea generation is something we have little control over. You're either an "idea person" or you're not, right?

Wrong.

Webb Young argues that the production of ideas follows a process as definite as the production of Fords; a process you can learn and practice.

Incidentally, James Webb Young was an advertising executive in the early-mid 1900s, which proves to some extent the value of this skill for copywriters.

And to pile on the proof, I have also observed Gary Halbert, one of the greatest copywriter's and marketing minds of all time, adopting this technique in his own work.

In one of his newsletters called *Hands-On Experience For A Basic Education In Advertising Principles*, The Prince Of Print explains how to go from no copywriting experience to a world-class promotion in 30 days.

Now, the reason I mention this here is that there's such an astonishing overlap in the process Gary recommended and the one James Webb Young published, that I wouldn't be surprised if Halbert adapted the process to his own work.

So, if one of the greatest ever copywriting and marketing minds used this technique to produce ideas for his own promotions… and if that same copywriter recommends using it to create an advertising promotion better than anybody you could hire (even if you've never written a word of copy) …

Then It's Probably Good Enough For You To Use!

Okay, enough. I think it's time to give you what you want and share the technique, isn't it?

But let me start with a caveat.

What follows is NOT a replacement for the James Webb Young book or the Gary Halbert newsletter. Frankly, I'm not fit to shine their shoes. If you are serious about generating ideas for your own or your client's advertising, then I strongly recommend you go directly to the source and read both. What follows is merely an introduction to the technique, plus one or two ideas for applying it to nutritional supplements advertising.

Okay, let's go!

Step 1: Gather your raw materials

Although it sounds obvious, most of us bypass the gathering of raw materials for creative activity. It's actually such a chore that, instead, we sit around waiting for inspiration to strike. Don't do that. As you'll see, inspiration will NOT strike. In fact, I propose that skipping this step is the main cause of "writer's block".

Webb Young said that there are two types of material to gather: general and specific.

Specific materials are those related to your product, your market and the people in it. So, what are general materials?

Gary Halbert recommended reading nine specific advertising books. I guess this was to give you a solid grounding in general advertising principles before focusing on your market and market.

But gathering general materials is an ongoing process. You should read and study other subjects because new ideas in advertising result from the combination of specific knowledge about products and people... with... general knowledge about life and events.

Is this why the late great Gene Schwartz insisted that every top copywriter should spend at least two ideas a day reading general material like newspapers and magazines?

Step 2: Work the raw materials over in your mind

If you have worked hard at gathering raw materials, it's time for the next step.

Mull over the information you have and stir it around in the giant mixing bowl of your mind.

Review all your notes, consider them carefully, say "hmm" every once in a while, look for the meaning, bring two facts together and see how they connect.

You are looking for a new relationship between previously independent facts or ideas. You will want to give up before long... but don't.

You will eventually reach the hopeless stage where your mind is all of a jumble and you are just not having any new insights.

Stop now and move on to step 3.

Step 3: Incubate the materials in your subconscious mind

This is my favorite step.

All you do is...

Nothing!

Drop the subject completely and make no effort of a direct nature.

Go and play golf for a few days.

Take some time off with your family.

Listen to music.

Go to the movies.

Do other work if you must; just don't work on your promotion.

Step 4: Eureka!

When Archimedes, the Greek scientist, stepped into the bath and noticed the water rise, he suddenly realized that the volume of water displaced must be equal to the volume of the body parts submerged.

Legend has it that Archimedes was so eager to share his discovery that he jumped out of the bath and ran naked through the streets of Athens shouting "Eureka!" ("I have found it" in Greek).

If you did steps 1-3 properly you will almost certainly experience this next step automatically.

Your subconscious mind will pop an idea into your consciousness, seemingly out of nowhere. You will have a eureka moment!

This is why we so often get ideas whilst taking a shower, shaving, walking the dog, etc. By relaxing the conscious mind, our subconscious has the energy to combine facts and spit new combinations into our consciousness.

When you have a Eureka moment, the next step is simple: WRITE!

Write. Write. Write. Write. And write some more.

Just lock the door to your office and get everything out. Do NOT censor yourself. Nobody is going to see what you write.

Your brain should be like an inflated balloon. It can only stretch so far and then it needs to release some air before it bursts.

What you will have after following these steps is a very rough starting point for your ad. You'll probably scrap most of it, but that doesn't matter, because there will also be some terrific ideas in there.

In the next chapter, you'll discover how to write each of the critical components of an effective supplement ad.

PART III:

WRITING YOUR AD

How To Find Your Big Idea

"You will never win fame and fortune unless you invent big ideas. It takes a big idea to attract the attention of consumers and get them to buy your product. Unless your advertising contains a big idea, it will pass like a ship in the night."

— David Ogilvy, Ogilvy on Advertising

In 1978, William "Bill" Bonner launched a small publishing company in Washington, DC.

That company is now known as Agora, Inc—one of the largest consumer newsletter publishers in the world.

Mark Ford, himself an esteemed copywriter and entrepreneur, credits Bonner with introducing the concept of the big idea into consumer direct marketing… and generating over a billion dollars as a result.

In fact, it was from Mark Ford that I first heard of the Big Idea whilst studying AWAI's accelerated copywriting program.

Keen to learn more, I found an article of Ford's where he told the story of meeting a group of Agora writer's with Bill Bonner.

The copywriters presented some leads they thought contained big ideas. But not a single one of them did. And try as they might, Ford and Bonner just could not get the copywriting stars to grasp the concept of a Big Idea.

So, if one of the greatest copywriters ever… and one of the most successful marketers of our time… could not explain this concept to a group of the best copywriter's in the world…

Then What In The Hell's Chance Do I Stand Of Successfully Explaining It To You?

Sod it, I'll do my best. And once you've finished this section, go and read Gary Halbert's newsletter, *The Big Idea*. It was reading this newsletter when the concept started to take shape in my own dull brain. Maybe, just maybe, the same will happen to you! Who knows?

Onward.

Here's an example of a big idea from the man himself, Mr. Bill Bonner. It's the lead for the first promotion he wrote for his *International Living* newsletter which ran as the control for almost 20 years. Here it is:

"You look out your window, past your gardener, who is busily pruning the lemon, cherry, and fig trees … amidst the splendor of gardenias, hibiscus, and hollyhocks.

The sky is clear blue. The sea is a deeper blue, sparkling with sunlight.

A gentle breeze comes drifting in from the ocean, clean and refreshing, as your maid brings you breakfast in bed.

For a moment, you think you have died and gone to heaven.

But this paradise is real. And affordable. In fact, it costs only half as much to live this dream lifestyle … as it would to stay in your own home!"

What's the big idea in there?

Well, it suggests that an exotic life overseas isn't just for the rich and famous; you can do it for less money than you currently live on. That's a big idea.

Now, let's go deeper and pick it apart, starting with a definition of the big idea from Mark Ford:

"A big idea is an idea that is instantly comprehended as important, exciting, and beneficial. It also leads to an inevitable conclusion, a conclusion that makes it easy to sell your product."

Here's what that means…

A big idea is important to the prospective customer and relevant to whatever is being sold.

In the example above, the letter aimed to sell its readers on a subscription to *International Living* magazine. So, do you think readers would be interested in the idea of living in paradise for less than they currently live on? YES, absolutely. And, this is exactly what the magazine shows them how to do.

A big idea is exciting.

You can't excite your customer by repeating ideas they have already heard over and over. Instead, you need to find a new angle that makes them sit up and pay attention. *International Living* did that incredibly well. The readers of that letter were so used to listening to the news and its negative stories that the idea of a happier, healthier and more exotic lifestyle… for less than they were currently spending… was certainly an exciting idea!

As well as being exciting, **the big idea must also provide a benefit to the prospect**.

In other words, it should make them want to buy the product. *International Living* could have got their audience excited by how the cost of living in the US was predicted to fall dramatically in the next few years, but that would have made them less likely to buy the product, not more.

Finally, what does Mark Ford mean by an **"inevitable conclusion"**? He means that a big idea must be simple and easy to understand. It must be easy to see how the product you are selling solves a particular problem. It should make the customer feel as though they need the product immediately, even before the product itself is mentioned in the copy. Here's another example...

"Want to slash strokes from your game almost overnight?

"Amazing Secret Discovered By One-Legged Golfer Adds 50 Yards To Your Drives, Eliminates Hooks and Slices ... And Can Slash Up To 10 Strokes From Your Game Almost Overnight!"

That's the headline for an ad written by John Carlton that ran profitably for many years. The big idea here—that there's a secret discovered by a one-legged golfer—is exciting, because it suggests that if the reader has two legs, he'd have an even greater advantage.

There's also a promise that the secret could add 50 yards to his drive and slash up to 10 strokes. This promise is both important and beneficial. To many passionate golfers, I'm sure they felt a burning desire to know this secret before they were even told how to get it... before they'd even read the opening paragraph, in fact!

Talking of John Carlton, his advice on finding a big idea is as simple and direct as you'll find.

In one of his products, he recommends going out and hunting for it. It won't find you, you'll have to do the research, study all the product materials you can get your hands on and talk to people in your market one-on-one.

In fact, I believe Carlton found the big idea for the golfing ad when talking to his client, who casually slipped into the conversation that he had once trained a one-legged golfer!

Lessons From The Most Stolen Library Book

Back when I was an aspiring copywriter, I knew that if I was going to be successful, I needed to study *Breakthrough Advertising*, the brilliant Eugene Schwartz book.

Problem was, it was no longer in print, used copies sold for upwards of $300, and I didn't have the money. Fortunately, the British Library managed to find a battered and bruised old copy.

Did you know that Boardroom positioned Breakthrough Advertising as "the most stolen library book"?

I'm not convinced of the accuracy of their claim, but I am ashamed to admit: I was very tempted to substantiate it.

After all, if I pretended I'd lost my copy, were they really going to charge me more than £300?

My conscience got the better of me in the end, but the reason I bring this up is that to get ahold of that library copy cost me £15. And I could only keep it for 7 days. That's quite a lot for a 7-day loan of a library book, don't you think?

Whatever.

I only had time to read it once. It's very dense and I only scratched the surface. But it was the best £15 I ever spent!

If you are serious about developing your chops as a copywriter, I strongly recommend reading, studying and re-reading it several times. And you won't have to steal a library copy because (at the time of writing, at least) it's back in print. You can buy a copy at breakthroughadvertisingbook.com.

Anyway, one of the most valuable ideas I took from my short read of *Breakthrough Advertising* is the concept of customer awareness. Here's how Eugene Schwartz explained it:

"If your prospect is aware of your product and realizes it can satisfy his desire, your headline starts with your product. If he is not aware of your product, but only of the desire itself, your headline starts with the desire. If he is not yet aware of what he really seeks but is concerned only with the general problem, your headline starts with that problem and crystallizes it into a specific need."

As you can see, Schwartz recommended changing how you approach the headline of an ad depending on the awareness of a typical prospect in your market.

Of course, everything starts with your headline, so I don't need to explain the importance of this concept any further.

Schwartz broke this down into what he called the "five levels of customer awareness".

Once you know which level your market is at, you can use it to make more effective marketing and copywriting decisions.

Before I show you how to do that, here's a brief explanation of each customer awareness level so you can decide where your prospects sit:

The Most Aware

The most aware prospects are those who know what they want, they know your business, they know your product, they know that your product is a solution to their problem, and all that's left is for them to hear "the deal".

This is the best type of customer. They are usually your raving fans. They buy a lot from you. They refer people to you. More often than not, all you need to do is offer them something valuable to buy and tell them the business proposition.

Product-Aware

These prospects know they have a problem, they know a solution exists, and they know about your product or service. They probably also know about the benefits of your product.

But they've not yet made up their minds about whether to buy your product. You'll need to earn their trust and avoid scaring them away.

Solution-Aware

Solution aware prospects know they have a problem, they know the result they want, but they don't know that your product or service provides it.

Problem-Aware

This stage is when a prospect knows he has a problem but doesn't know there's a solution. They know that something isn't working, and they are worried about it, but they don't know there's a way to fix it.

Completely Unaware

This category contains prospects who don't know who you are, don't know your product, and don't know products like yours even exist. And, they don't know they have a specific problem that's worth solving.

Onward.

The first step in using the concept of customer awareness to improve your copy is to ask yourself,

"Which level of awareness is a typical prospect?"

Then...

The more aware your prospect is, the more direct you should make your lead.

If your prospect is in the most aware stage, for instance, they don't need to be educated and taken to the offer slowly. They just want to know what the deal is. You can go right ahead and make a direct offer in the headline.

For example:

"FREE—The Book That Has Helped Thousands to Get Slim and Stay Slim"

"Now… Paleo Power IN A PILL!"

"THE FINEST NUTRITIONAL SUPPLEMENTS MONEY CAN BUY!"

"THE $23c LIFE-SAVER Heart Surgeons NEVER Tell You About!"

"Hands that look lovelier in 24 hours—or your money back"

But what if your prospect is at the opposite end of the spectrum, in the completely unaware stage?

Then a direct offer like this would most likely repel them. Direct leads give away the advertiser's intention to sell something. The most aware prospects are happy about that because they know they have a problem, they know your product can solve it, and they just want to hear your proposition. But the least aware customers, remember, don't even know they have a problem worth solving. So, to them, a direct lead is just an uninteresting sales pitch.

Here are a few examples of indirect headlines:

"71-Year Old Man Has Sexual Congress 5 Times a Day"

"Boom! Your Explosive Gut Is About To Go Off..."

"Age 80 is the new 50!"

"How did THEY do it? Real-Life Stories of Healing & "Aging in Reverse..." in Their Own Words"

"How to live 42 percent longer... and still eat loads of cheese, breads, cream sauces, and rich desserts!"

"Every year, the U.S. Medical System kills more than 770,000 people. That's like seven jumbo jets falling from the sky and crashing every day."

Here's a simple way to measure the directness of an ad: the quicker it mentions the product and the business proposition, the more direct it is.

Okay, how does this apply to writing ads for nutritional supplements?

Well, Eugene Schwartz also wrote about something called market sophistication. He proposed that the directness of your ad should be influenced by how many similar products your prospects have seen before—how often they've been sold to.

Without going into the details, which I really can't do justice here, the reason I bring it up is that 99% of the time, when you are selling nutritional supplements, your prospect is in a later stage of sophistication.

They've seen similar products before. They receive regular direct mail and other promotions. There's a good chance they've learned to distrust advertisers, having bought supplements and not received the benefits they were promised.

What this means is simple: leads that offer a straight benefit or mention the product or deal too early will rarely work in health markets.

Instead, it's much better to lead by capturing the problem and its associated pains. Connect with the reader on an emotional level way before you mention anything about your product.

If you want more information on how to write leads based on market awareness and sophistication, then I'll refer you to another outstanding resource: *Great Leads* by Michael Masterson and John Forde. It builds on *Breakthrough Advertising* and walks you through six different types of lead with varying degrees of directness.

No Read, No Sale

Let's talk envelopes.

This small rectangular piece of paper can be the difference between a sales letter that brings in the big bucks… and a sales letter which completely flops.

Here's why: if your letter never gets read, it cannot possibly sell anything! So, the first job of a sales letter… is simply…

To Get Read!

And to get read, the recipient first needs to open the envelope and look at the contents. With this in mind, most mail order advertisers use teaser copy.

One promotion from Prevention Health Books, Rodale, Inc. (a prolific mailer and tester) features the following copy on the envelope:

"Look Great! Feel Fabulous! I'm 45. A working mother of two. And if I can be in my best shape ever, so can you!"

This particular envelope also features more copy and an image of workout guru, Denise Austin.

The idea of teaser copy, of course, is to tease you so much about what's inside the envelope that you can't resist opening and reading the message. This particular promotion is highly successful. But assuming you are not an expert mailer like Rodale who has a handful of world's best "A-list" copywriters at your fingertips... then writing teaser copy on your envelope's will almost certainly harm your results.

And the reason why is contained in Gary Halbert's semi-famous "A-pile, B-pile" teaching. As The Prince of Print explains in chapter 11 of his book, *The Boron Letters*, most people divide their mail into two piles.

The first pile, the "A-pile", is anything they deem to be personal correspondence. The second pile, the "B-pile", is anything that looks commercial.

Once they have divided their mail into these two piles, what do they do?

Well, everybody wants to read their personal mail, so the first thing they do is set their "B" pile aside and get on with reading everything in their "A" pile.

Once they've finished the "A" pile, what do they do with the "B" pile? Does it ever get opened? Yes, sometimes it gets opened... but only IF the person has some spare time... IF they are bored... and IF it looks interesting. Only then MIGHT they open the "B" pile mail. But often...

It Just Gets Thrown Straight In The Trash!

And so, the problem with teaser copy is that it sends an immediate signal to the recipient that the envelope in their hand does NOT contain personal information... but DOES contain an advertisement.

Unless the teaser copy really is world-class (and sometimes even if it is) ... that envelope is destined for the trash. No good!

It should be painfully apparent that... if only half the people who receive your letter open it... then only half have an opportunity to even read your promotion and get an opportunity to buy.

Clearly, then, the first job of a direct mail promotion is to get the envelope into the "A" pile. And, although this secret is so frequently overlooked, it is really very simple to achieve. All you need to do is...

Make It Look Like Personal Mail!

Alright, enough build up. Here's exactly what to do:

1. Use plain white or manila 6x9 or 9x12 envelopes

2. Have the address typed

3. NO TEASER COPY

4. Use an "URGENT" or "PERSONAL AND CONFIDENTIAL" stamp if you want

5. Do not put your name, business name, or a P.O. box in the corner

6. Use a real, live first-class stamp.

How To Write A Killer Headline

Which of the following two headlines do you think was successful?

They were both tested in an advertisement selling a course of treatments for people with nervous ailments. Here they are:

1. "Thousands suffer from sick nerves and don't know it"

2. "Have you these symptoms of nerve exhaustion?"

So, which do you think pulled the best?

Okay, I'll tell you.

Headline 1 was unsuccessful, headline 2 was successful. Why? Because headline 1 contains the word "you", and therefore arouses curiosity. It also suggests a remedy for nervous problems.

Headline 2, on the other hand, is simply a statement of fact.

But here's what is so insightful about this little exercise: both of these headlines were considered good enough to test by the advertiser.

Significant sums of money were spent to find out which one would work. And, in performing these tests, they both had the same offer…

"Please send me a copy of your book, "New Nerves for Old." I am enclosing 50 cents in coin or stamps."

In fact, in these tests, everything else about the advertisement was kept exactly the same. Which means that…

The Headline <u>Alone</u> Can Be The Difference Between A Winner And A Loser!

The late Eugene Schwartz, one of the greatest ever copywriter's, would beat the control package his copy was tested against over 85% of the time. But even he said that, when another copywriter came up with a headline that was beyond belief, their ad would almost always win against any others that ran against it.

Perhaps that's why the great Claude Hopkins was known to test headlines nearly 2000 times for a single product.

He observed, over many years and millions spent on advertising tests, that a change in headline can multiply returns by 5 or 10 times.

In fact, as you saw in the example above, it can be the difference between a successful and unsuccessful ad.

Indeed, it matters naught what the rest of your ad says or offers if you cannot get your target audience to read the ad in the first place.

Have I successfully persuaded you of the importance of the headline?

Good!

Then let's move on to the nitty-gritty... how to write a headline.

But first, based on the above, can you see what the job of a headline is? A headline has just two jobs: (1) capture the attention on your intended audience, and (2) persuade them to read the next line.

Nothing more, nothing less. It doesn't have to sell anything...

... it doesn't have to be restricted to 5 words or 1 line...

... it doesn't have to be (and shouldn't be) cutesy or clever...

... the only thing it has to do is capture the attention of your intended audience... and persuade them to read the next line.

But it must do these two jobs quickly. You have less than a second before your prospect decides whether to continue reading or throw your letter in the bin (or skip past your ad) and continue on merrily with their day.

You know, there's a lot of hype about copywriting formulas. The most useful for headlines, in my opinion, is the "Four U's" formula.

The idea is that each of the U's describes a critical part of a headline. And, when put together they hook your prospect's interest, entice them with a benefit, establish credibility, and urge them to continue reading. Here are the "Four-U's":

Urgency: give the reader a reason to desire the benefit quickly

Usefulness: communicate something of value to the prospect

Uniqueness: suggest that whatever is being offered is in some way different from everything else of its type

Ultra-specificity: communicate to the reader what specific benefits are in store for them.

Okay, now for the caveat: it's very easy to get overwhelmed when writing headlines. There are so many different ways to do it and every copywriter you ask will tell you a different way. Perhaps that's why headline formulas exist. People want a quick fix for something difficult.

More importantly, using formula's for headlines will only get you so far. And the reason is that your headline has to connect with your specific target audience. Formula's don't account for that. To write a great headline, you have to understand the pains, fears, and desires of your intended audience.

How else can you expect to get their attention and connect with them?

Once you can do that, you won't need a formula. So, to avoid getting overwhelmed by the hundreds of different ways to write headlines, I would highly recommend that you simply get to know your intended readers inside out and write a headline that you know would get their attention and interest them enough to read the next line.

Right, here are a few more ways to increase the power of your headline…

Use your prospect's name

Jim Farley, the politician who helped Franklin D. Roosevelt win the Presidency, told Dale Carnegie—in his book *How to Win Friends and Influence People*—that the secret to his success was that he could call 50,000 people by their first name.

Carnegie went on to explain that calling a person by their name gives them a feeling of importance. And how a feeling of importance is one of the primary human desires. You can use this to your advantage in headlines.

Simply, if you know their name, use it! It is practically guaranteed to get their attention and persuade them to read what you have to say.

In fact, using your prospect's name in the headline can increase response by as much as 30%!

Use trigger words

If you don't have the name of your prospect—let's say, because you are writing a magazine ad—then use "trigger words".

Trigger words are short and very direct descriptions of the thing your prospects are interested in. Here is a classic example from the health market:

"Sneaky Little Arthritis Tricks, Natural Foods and Do-It-Yourself Secrets That Pain-Proofed Over 100 Men and Women Like You."

If you were suffering from arthritis, would respond to words like arthritis, do-it-yourself, and pain-proofed?

Make it as long as necessary

A headline should be as short as possible, right?

Wrong.

Well, sort of.

You see, a headline should be as long as it needs to be to stop your intended reader and get them going, and no more.

It's foolish to restrict yourself to a 5-word headline that does its job poorly but, it's also foolish to say in 20 words what you could say just as effectively in 7.

Cite institutions like Harvard and Yale

If you can cite well-respected institutions in your headline and make it work in the context of the rest of your ad, it's a very powerful way to get someone's attention and develop immediate credibility.

My favorite health market example is a letter mailed by a publisher on behalf of John Hopkins Medicine, the world-famous hospital. The letter starts off with:

"Direct to you from John Hopkins Medicine" …

… followed by their logo and the headline:

"You've been chosen to receive a free issue of Health After 50 because living longer is only half the goal."

Onward.

When you sit down to start writing your headlines, here's a great way to get started:

Gather all your research in a document. Read it. Add thoughts of your own. Be wordy. Just write.

Then, when you have completed getting your thoughts down, stop.

Read the block of text you've just written. There will probably be a sentence or two in there with a good idea. **Bold it**. Then write some headlines using the bold sentences. Keep going. Just write.

Before long, you'll have a bunch of headlines on the page.

Remember: this is confidential. Nobody else but you need see your list of headlines. So get everything out. It doesn't matter if they're any good or not.

Just write!

The Best Way To Write An Opening Paragraph

According to David Ogilvy, five times as many people read the headline as read the body copy.... and if your headline is no good, you have wasted 90% of your advertising money.

It follows then, that the headline is the most important element of an ad. So, what is the second most important element?

Some claim it is the postscript; the P.S. They say a prospect will read the headline, then read the P.S., and then decide whether to read the rest of the ad. The P.S. is certainly important... but is it the second most important part of the ad?

I'm not so sure. It seems logical to me that if the headline is good—by our definition in the last section, that means it grabs the attention of the intended reader... and... persuades them to read the next line—then it is surely true that the next most important part of the ad is: the next line.

And after the headline comes the opening paragraph.

If you are writing a personal communication like a sales letter, then the salutation comes first. But this is sometimes omitted, for example, in magazine ads. If you do use a salutation, the best approach is simple:

use the recipient's name. If not, just use "Dear Friend".

Onward to the opening paragraph.

First, a little teaser: what do you think are the two most powerful words in advertising?

Fortunately, Gary Bencivenga, widely considered the world's greatest living copywriter, wrote a superb "bullet" on his website on this very subject.

Most people, he said, assume that the two most powerful words are FREE and NEW. And in "the old days", they might well have been. But, both of those words have been so overused that all they do is sound a very loud alarm in the reader's mind.

Yes, they trigger a response. But not the response you want. Not a sale... but the thought: YEAH, SURE.

Yeah, sure. The two most powerful words in advertising—according to the man whose ads have run in over $1 billion of scientific direct response marketing tests over a 40-year period—are "yeah, sure."

And the reason why should be obvious. It is simply this: if your ad stimulates a "yeah, sure" reaction in your prospect... they are more likely to throw it in the wastebasket than buy from you.

Right, let's talk about how to avoid the "yeah, sure" reaction.

The most obvious solution is to avoid the overused words and phrases that trigger the reaction. In health markets, there's "lose weight fast". Yeah, sure.

There's also "free", "new" and "get rich quick". Yeah, sure.

But the real solution to this problem, which according to Gary Bencivenga is often what separates the tiny handful of A-level copywriter's, is…

You Should Never Make Your Claim Bigger Than Your Proof!

There are so many ways to achieve this, but I'm in danger of going off on a tangent.

So, the real reason for me bring this up is that one way to avoid the yeah, sure reaction… and… make your proof bigger than your claim is to…

"Sandwich your big promise inside an IF… THEN construction".

The formula is simple: a reasonably easy requirement, followed by a strong promise. Bencivenga recommended using it in your headline but, you can also use it for your opening paragraph (hence my writing about it here).

It's an opening paragraph style which Gary Halbert used a lot. Here are some examples from his ads:

"If you'd like to lose weight... for real... and... do it extremely fast (up to 10 pounds of fat and fluid in 2 days... then... up to 1 pound a day until you reach your goal) this is going to be the most exciting message you'll ever read!"

"If you are already a professional model, or, if you'd like to be, this is going to be the most exciting message you will ever read. On the other hand, if you want to be a model... but... you don't really have what it takes... this message can save you thousands of dollars and a great deal of misery and heartbreak."

"If you have a weight problem, I want you to take a good look at the pictures on this page."

"If you are interested in living a very long life... and... staying young and healthy... this will be the most important message you will ever read."

Okay, here's a little bonus for you—a way to make the "if...then" opener even more powerful. You can do this by... simply... adding some proof.

Here's an example:

"If you want to learn how to add 10 pounds of muscle in 30 days then this is how the Navy SEALs do it... and how you can too."

Notice how adding "this is how the Navy SEALs do it" makes the claim so much more believable?

Here are some other ways to write opening paragraphs...

The Candor Opener

Example: "My name is Betty Adams and the first thing you should know about me is... I am not a doctor. I'm not an expert on nutrition either. I never went to college and I don't have a degree in anything. In fact, the only thing I consider myself an "expert" about is..."

The "Did You Know" Opener

Example: "Did you know the quality of your smile has a more direct effect on your personal (and business) relationships than any other part of your appearance?"

The Bite-Size Opener

Examples: "I was the total skeptic" and "Picture this..."

The Grabber Opener

A "grabber" is something you attach to a direct mail letter that grabs the reader's attention. Naturally, your opening paragraph has to explain why you have done this, and how it relates to the rest of your letter.

Example:

"As you can see, I am sending you a $1.00 bill with this letter. I'm doing this for a reason: This is the most important letter you will ever read, and I needed some way to make sure this letter would catch your attention.

And, quite frankly, there is ANOTHER reason I am sending you this dollar bill. I'll tell you the other reason in a minute... but first... there is a strange story I have to tell you. In fact, I've got to get this off my chest before I explode!"

The Question Opener

Example: "Do you ever have pain in your knees?"

The Sensationalist Opener

Example: "Let's talk about how the size of a woman's breasts relates to her I.Q."

Are these the only ways you can write an opening paragraph? No, certainly not. In fact, the only thing your opening paragraph needs to do is… grab the readers interest so effectively that they can't help but read the next section.

The Top Gun School Of Persuasion

In one of his products, Ben Settle—the world leader in email copywriting education— told a story about the classic movie, Top Gun.

If you haven't seen it, here's the low-down: it's about a cocky, Ray-Ban-wearing fighter pilot called Maverick (played by Tom Cruise) whose mission it is to "top" the class of the Top Gun Naval Fighter Weapons School… and… win over his beautiful instructor.

When the movie was released, two surprising (and presumably unintentional) things happened…

1. Sales of Ray-Ban Aviator's exploded

2. Interest in joining the U.S. Air Force grew so quickly they positioned recruitment stands inside movie theatre's where Top Gun was showing

Now, nowhere in the movie were Ray-Ban sunglasses advertised. Nowhere in the movie was the U.S. Air Force actively promoted.

No… it was the story of Top Gun, and the vision and aura of Maverick's life, that did the selling.

The point is: not only do we love reading and listening to stories… they are an incredibly influential sales tool.

It's almost like we are hard-wired to read, absorb, listen to, and be persuaded by stories. And, they work especially well in supplement promotions.

Why?

Because people experience highly-charged, emotional health dramas… and they want a solution from somebody who can empathize with their pain.

When they learn that others have experienced the same suffering as they have and successfully overcome it, they gain hope that they too can manage their health problem successfully.

That's why inspirational stories are especially powerful in the health market.

Not just in your ad… but also in your emails and other content. No matter how happy anyone says they are, there's always a hidden dream tucked away deep inside. We all harbor secret fantasies of elaborate lives.

Inspirational stories allow us to indulge in them and warm us up to take action. And inspiring ACTION is very useful in sales copy, is it not?

Short story long: stories give you the power to get the reader nodding along in agreement, all the way to the order form.

Righty-o!

There's a lot to learn about storytelling, but for the sake of writing a good supplement ad, let's keep it simple (you can read up on deep storytelling theory later if you want).

Here are four basic story types you can use.

A story about you

From a Gary Halbert ad:

"My name is Gary Halbert and, some time ago, I was dead broke. My business was almost bankrupt, and I couldn't even pay the rent. Actually, I wasn't just broke, I was desperate. Then, one day, I came up with a "crazy idea" about how to write a certain kind of sales letter (it was not a chain letter) that would get people to send me money."

If you are selling a supplement, and your reason for selling it is that it first benefitted you in some way, then consider telling your before and after story.

A story about someone else

The Institute for Vibrant Living published a successful ad which detailed real-life, personal, "Aging in Reverse" stories. It started:

"Behind the scenes of a medical breakthrough... How did THEY do it? Real-Life Stories of Healing & Aging in Reverse..." in their own words"

This approach was also used by Rodale, Inc., a hugely successful health publisher and direct response marketer. According to their star copywriter at the time, Eugene Schwartz, they were having trouble selling a book about arthritis. See, doctors wrote most Rodale books—which is, of course, what people want… health information from a recognized expert.

But this particular book wasn't written by a doctor. It featured 766 people who had cured their arthritis themselves by means the doctors didn't agree with. Schwartz realized that the reason people weren't buying the book was that they were sneaking around behind their doctors' backs to find a solution… and they felt guilty about it. So, he came up with the headline:

"Sneaky Little Arthritis Tricks, Natural Foods and Do-It-Yourself Secrets That Pain-Proofed Over 100 Men and Women Like You."

The headline… the ad… and the product itself… all told a story about other people. It pulled like crazy.

A parable

A parable is a story with a moral lesson; a simple narrative that illustrates a universal truth. Rather than give you a specific example, find a bible and turn to any page. Entire religions were built on parables… which tells you a lot about their influence.

A historical story

Historical stories are used a lot in health copy. Here's a snippet from a long-running control by Advanced BioNutritionals:

"… but although this superfood is virtually unknown in the West, it's been around for over 2,000 years. In fact, Himalayan guides, or Sherpas, have relied on it for centuries to fight fatigue, boost energy, and build endurance…"

Vision Drives Decision

Once upon a time, the FBI faced a hostage crisis in the Philippines. The negotiation went badly… and two people died.

When an FBI agent was traveling home from Manilla, he landed in Washington and spotted a negotiation book authored by Jim Camp.

The agent was so impressed and intrigued by what he read… … that Jim Camp was contacted by the FBI… … and ended up helping them build a training package for their hostage crisis negotiators.

The FBI even went on record saying that Jim Camp created the biggest revolution in negotiation in the last 50 years.

Short story long, Jim Camp was not just the world's most feared negotiator…

He Was A Master Of Persuasion!

I'd highly recommend studying Jim Camp's work, but for the purpose of this message, Camp's philosophy on negotiation could be summed up in three words:

"Vision Drives Decision"

My favorite example of this is the speech Winston Churchill gave to the House of Commons on June 4, 1940.

It was the most troubled time in our history; the darkest hour of World War 2 (great movie by the way, "The Darkest Hour"). When practically the entire British Army were enclosed by Nazi troops in Dunkirk, a German invasion of Britain looked imminent.

Civilian morale was at rock bottom. Churchill had no support from his own war cabinet to fight back— they all wanted to negotiate with Hitler.

So, Churchill was tasked with delivering a speech which told the public the truth about the great military disaster at Dunkirk and warned them of a possible German invasion attempt, without casting doubt on eventual victory.

Here is a segment of his famous speech to the House of Commons:

"We shall go on to the end. We shall fight in France. We shall fight on the seas and oceans, we shall fight with growing confidence and growing strength in the air, we shall defend our island, whatever the cost may be.

We shall fight on the beaches, we shall fight on the landing grounds, we shall fight in the fields and in the streets, we shall fight in the hills; we shall NEVER SURRENDER, and if, which I do not for a moment believe, this island or a large part of it were subjugated and starving, then our Empire beyond the seas, armed and guarded by the British fleet, would carry on the struggle, until, in God's good time, the New World, with all its power and might, steps forth to the rescue and a liberation of the old."

Churchill could easily have told the public that Belgium and other countries had already surrendered, that the Germans were close to conquering Western Europe and to expect an invasion any day.

Instead, he created a vision of German troops landing on the beaches and in the hills, and the British people fighting them off with all their might.

He also painted the picture of Canada, the United States, Australia, New Zealand, India and other allies coming to Britain's rescue if and when they needed it.

This proved to be a great turning point in the war... with the allies battling to victory five years later.

My point is that painting a vision of the future allows people to make a decision. It is an incredibly powerful persuasive tool in negotiation... in war... and in copy.

You can use words on a page, as Churchill did with his speech, to capture your reader's imagination, and paint pleasing pictures of what your product will do for them.

And there's actually a simple, structured way to approach this.

First, you make an extensive list of all the "features" of your product. Do you know what a feature is? I prefer to call it a "fact". It is simply a fact about your product.

Create a fact sheet which contains every detail of your product. Don't place any limitations on this list. Be exhaustive. It doesn't matter if a fact doesn't seem relevant; just get it down.

What is the name of your supplement?

What is the name of each ingredient?

What quantity of each ingredient does the product contain?

How did you make it?

What form does it take? Pill? Liquid?

How should your customer take the supplement? Okay, you get the idea.

This list of facts, by the way, is where most writer's stop when presenting a product to prospective customers. Big mistake. The reader still has lots of questions in their mind when reading about the facts of a product.

Say you sell a supplement which contains the ingredient whey protein. The customer still wants to know...

"Is whey the best type of protein to take?"

"Can I taste the whey—it doesn't sound very nice?"

"Where does whey protein come from?"

"Is whey protein any good?"

So, once you've got a long fact sheet together—10 pages or more—it's time to answer your reader's questions by attaching a "benefit" to each fact.

A benefit, in copywriting lingo, is simply…

What The Thing DOES For The Person Using It!

Eugene Schwartz called it a "does-y". It's your functional product. Some examples:

Not just a puppy… … a puppy that licks your face when you get home from work.

Not just a 3-liter turbo engine… … a 3-liter turbo engine that roars like a lion when you turn the ignition and zips past vehicles with the slightest depression of the accelerator pedal.

Not just whey protein… … whey protein that starts repairing (and growing) your muscles 3 minutes post-consumption.

Not just calcium… … calcium to strengthen your bones and reduce your risk of fracture.

Get the idea?

Okay, try to attach a benefit to every fact, and do this until you have a long and extensive "benefit list".

Again, make this as long as you can.

What you are doing here is answering the questions in your reader's mind. Explain yourself, but don't be boring. Do it in a way that...

Captures Their Imagination And Paints Pleasing Pictures In Their Mind!

And, the way you do this is by using action verbs. Most copywriters rely on adjectives to get their point across. But great copy is light on adjectives and heavy on action verbs.

The great John Carlton takes this a step further with what he calls "power words". Power words include verbs that convey action, but also include nouns with shock value or a powerful phrase like a twist on a cliché. Power words and phrases carry their own emotional wallop. They reach out from the page and grab you by the lapels. They get your blood pumping and paint vivid pictures in your mind.

Here are some examples:

Outrage... Humiliate... Force-feed... Stagger... Murder... Crave... Conquer... Dog-eared... Sick as a dog... Unbelievably devastating... Dragged kicking and screaming... Bone-crunching... Freak out... Line your pocket... Jackpot... Honest-to-God... Butt-ugly.

Finally, the meaty part of your ad… the place where you can really ignite your reader's desire… is where you list your facts and benefits. And, the best way to present them is with bullets.

Now, there are many different types of bullets you can write. Here are just a few:

Curiosity:

"Bills it's okay to pay late"

Who wouldn't want to know which bills they can get away with paying late?

Can't be done:

"How to buy a house with no down payment"

This seems ALMOST impossible. Yet, it's believable enough to make you want to know the secret.

Proof and credibility:

"How to put The Times in its place—as accomplished by such masters as Spiro Agnew, Ralph Bunche, Roy Innis, Lyndon Johnson, Karl Mundt, Robert F. Kennedy, Richard M. Nixon, Mrs. Leonard Bernstein, and others less famous but equally outspoken"

This is from an ad selling a book on getting a letter published by The New York Times. The bullet uses famous names to provide credibility to the claim that the reader will learn how to put The Times "in its place".

Contrast:

"Why copying the great golfers may be ruining your game (see page 168)"

How would copying great golfers ruin your game? Surely it would make you better...?

Straight benefit:

"How to keep sour cream from burning when you cook with it. See page 23."

This is taken from an ad selling "The Chef's Secret Cook Book". The bullet simply offers a solution to a problem the market has.

Okay, here are some health examples:

• "Little-known herbal supplement has "100% success rate" for clearing up bladder infections! (And, nope, it's NOT cranberry juice.)"

• "Doctors are now using this hot new herbal compound to slow the memory loss of Alzheimer's more effectively than expensive, dangerous prescription drugs!

• "The amazing 'Towel Hanging' trick that increases the strength of your erection ... plus your lovemaking stamina ... allowing you to supercharge your love life in a very short time! (You have to rience these kinds of 'rocket-burst' orgasms to believe they're possible! See page 139.)"

• "New all-natural way to increase serotonin (the brain chemical that fights depressions) works just like Prozac… minus the drowsiness and brain-fog!"

• "If you need to shed a few extra pounds, but hate to diet, then see page 184. You'll learn to eat as much as you do now yet burn more calories. And no exercise required!"

• "Erase back pain with your own hands. Massaging these acupressure points triggers a flood of painkilling endorphins. Page 71."

• "Eat your way to healthy arteries. What could be better? These delicious, flavonoid-rich foods flush out arterial cholesterol and plaque while you savor every bite. Page 156."

• "Lubricate creaky knees from within! Special exercise unleashes a flood of soothing synovial fluid into tired, stiff knees! Page 174."

• "Beat allergies with salsa! That's right—spicy foods will help break up the mucus, aid breathing and reduce allergy agony. But avoid these other popular foods that are guaranteed to make your allergies worse! See page 157."

The last bullet about beating allergies is a great example of a "one-two punch" bullet—a term coined by the great John Carlton.

It's a one-two punch because it gives a benefit… and then another benefit. A jab to wake him up… followed by a ruthless hook to really bring it home.

Notice also that the first sentence gives a secret away. Eating salsa and spicy foods reduces allergy symptoms.

But the second sentence is a "blind" bullet. You get a clear picture of the benefit you will receive from the product—in this case by reading page 157—but no idea what the exact secret is.

The reader knows they should steer clear of certain popular foods… but they don't know which foods! To get the answer, they need to buy the product.

Can you see how this works? Good.

Okay, one final tip. When you've written your bullets and you are assembling the many pieces of your ad…

Put Your Two Best Bullets First And Last In The List!

Skimmers tend to read the first and last bullets before deciding whether to go back and read the rest. This gives you the best possible chance of persuading them to continue reading. And you DO want them to read the bullets… it's where most of the selling happens!

How To Close The Sale

What is the purpose of a sales letter?

Of course, it is to sell your product or service to your intended audience; the reader. But the purpose of the letter is not to make a sale at some non-specific point in the future.

It is not to build awareness of your brand in the hope that the reader will someday decide to seek you out.

No, NO, NO!

The purpose of a sales letter is to persuade the reader to take action ***immediately***.

People, by and large, postpone and procrastinate… and postponed action is often forgotten. So, if your prospect decides to "go and think about it" … then you've lost.

You must get him to act RIGHT NOW!

There are many ways to get action, none of which can be applied universally to every ad. So, my intention here is not to impart on to you a specific technique or method for getting action. Instead, it is to provide a structure you can adapt to your own ads. Here it is:

1. Create an offer no sane person can refuse

2. Erase all trace of risk

3. Light a fire under his ass

4. Make it crazy simple to order

If you've been paying attention, you've already learned how to develop an irresistible offer and a risk-reversal guarantee.

The next step is to create a level of urgency on par with the reader's house being on fire. They have five minutes to get out... or else.

Similarly, your task is to make them feel as though they must act without a second's delay to get their hands on your incredible solution. They will never have the opportunity again. Ever. Just give them a believable reason why. For example...

"There are only 231 bottles left... and I expect them to sell out by Thursday. And when they're gone, they're gone."

"Last time we offered this deal, we sold out in 24 hours. Don't miss out—if you wait even another day, you won't have another chance at this full price for a full year."

"I can make this offer for the next 7 days ONLY. After that, the price goes back up forever."

The key is that it has to be believable.

In his book, *My Life In Advertising*, Claude Hopkins told the story of a clothing company on the verge of bankruptcy.

They called in an advertising writer with a stellar reputation—a man named John Powers—to help rescue them.

"Tell the truth. Tell the people you are bankrupt and that your only way to salvation lies through large and immediate sales," Powers recommended.

They were reluctant, of course, but Powers insisted. They eventually caved, and ran an ad that went something like this:

"We are bankrupt. We owe $115,000, more than we can pay. This announcement will bring our creditors down on our necks. But if you come and buy tomorrow, we shall have the money to meet them. If not, we go to the wall. These are the prices we are quoting to meet this situation…"

The effect was incredible.

People flocked in their thousands to the store… and the clothing company was saved. The reason, Hopkins contended, was that truth in advertising was so rare that the announcement caused a sensation.

This example also provides helpful insight into persuading your reader to act immediately. It shows, quite simply, that people respond when they truly believe what you say to them.

This particular ad was so spectacularly honest that it would, surely, have been ridiculous for the advertiser to make it up.

This is the effect you should aim for when crafting a persuasive close. Yes, give them a reason to act immediately. But make it so honest and believable that your reader has no reason to question your integrity.

Finally, now your prospect has cash in hand, ready to buy… your job is to make it so fast, easy and painless to order that the entire process is over in the blink of an eye.

If you take phone orders, make sure there's always somebody there to take the order. And tell your customer exactly what to say when they call.

If you use an order card/form, make sure you include all essential information—shipping information, your address and phone number, price details, the offer, and your guarantee. And, make sure you key-code the order form so you know where the order came from.

It also pays to include a summary of your sales message on the order form, so you don't lose your prospect at the final hurdle.

Always remember: the closer someone is to handing over their hard-earned money, the more objections run through their mind.

Counter their objections, remove the risks, and encourage them to take action one final time.

One more thing.

Here are some specific techniques you can use that work particularly well in nutritional supplement copy.

The False Close

Just when your prospect thinks you are going to ask for money, introduce a new benefit or offer another premium. This helps to remove objections. Then, you can lead them through the close... all the way to the sale.

Future Pacing

1. Show your prospect where he is right now

2. Take him forward in time, to a moment when he's used your product to reach a desirable outcome

3. Acknowledge this future outcome

This closing technique is massively under-utilized in health copy. So, use it to your competitive advantage.

The Takeaway

The more you tell your customer this may NOT be for them, the more they'll want it. It's a weird quirk of human psychology. I guess, the less accessible something is, the more value a person places on it... and the more they want it.

You can implement this by being honest and transparent about who your product is NOT for. No need to pretend or be arrogant.

I don't believe there is a product or service in existence that's right for everybody, even in a tiny market. There are always conditions a prospect has to meet to be a good fit. For example, if you sell a supplement that eases arthritis symptoms...

... do you really want people who haven't been diagnosed with arthritis to buy it?

How about people with severe, advanced arthritis who you KNOW wouldn't notice any change in their symptoms?

So, just be honest.

Simply say, "This is not for you if...", then be sincere and list the disqualification criteria for your supplement.

PART IV:

EDITING YOUR AD

Word By Word

You know, I think most people assume that great writers sit down at their desk every morning feeling on top of the world.

They roll their sleeves up, perhaps write a few rough sentences to get started, and they're off to the races, gushing out their creative genius.

I think this misleading belief is a cause of the so-called writer's block.

Writer's put so much pressure on themselves to sit down and produce the final piece, that they simply can't get anything out.

When they do get words down, when they aren't very good, it's frustrating. And the more frustrated they get, the harder it is to write.

In her terrific book, *Bird By Bird*, author Anne Lamott points out that for most, writing is not such a heavenly experience as one might assume…

"In fact, the only way I can get anything written at all is to write really, really shitty first drafts."

The first draft is where you let your inner child come out and just write whatever comes to your mind. No one is going to see it; you can edit later.

Stephen King is one of the most prolific writers ever. At the time of writing, he has published over 59 novels, 5 non-fiction books, and written a further 200 plus short stories. His books have sold more than 350 million copies. King writes incredibly fast—at least 2000 words a day—and says:

"The first draft of a book—even a long one— should take no more than three months, the length of a season."

Presumably, King subscribes to the idea of not censoring yourself on the first draft, and just getting as much down as possible.

So, if it's most productive to write the first draft of your ad as quickly as possible, it stands to reason that editing is also a significant part of the process.

To borrow from Anne Lamott's book title, editing —not writing—is the time to take it word by word.

How To Edit

Once you've written your shitty first draft, it's time to turn it into a persuasive sales message.

Just like sitting down to write, taking the first step in editing can be overwhelming.

Here's how to approach it.

Imagine for a moment that your ad is like a tree. Every sentence is a branch on that tree. And every word is a leaf on a branch. First comes the tree itself; the overall structure of your ad. Then comes the branch; the structure of the sentence. Then you see the leaves popping up. They give the branch color and strength and power.

Now, if you spend all of your time selecting the right words, but there is no structure to your ad, then it will be ineffective at making a sale.

Equally, if you get the structure right but the message and words themselves don't resonate, then again, it's unlikely to be persuasive.

The best way to approach editing, in my experience at least, is to get the overall structure right first. Then, zoom in and rejig the sentences. And finally, zoom in some more and focus on individual words.

Structure

The first thing I want you to do is to take your first draft and rearrange it into the following structure:

1. A headline that gets attention

2. Use a personal salutation (if you can)

3. Tell the reader who you are and why you are writing to them

4. Tell them why they should believe you

5. Prove that what you are saying is true

6. List and describe all of the benefits (in bullets)

7. State your offer

8. Tell them how to order

9. Tell them to order now (and why)

10. Add a P.S. with glowing testimonials

11. Include an order form

12. Code your ad for tracking (or an online equivalent)

Next, here are three specific ways you can arrange the body copy of a supplement ad.

1. By ingredient

You can organize supplement copy from the most to the least important ingredient. Once you know which ingredient is most important, based on its benefits to the reader, use more space to explain it than the others.

2. By market

You can also organize your copy by the market. If your product has five different benefits, start with the one that will appeal to the largest number of prospects.

3. By health needs

The more severe a particular problem is to your prospect, and the quicker they need to solve it, the more powerful an appeal to solve that problem is likely to be. Start by listing the health problems your supplement can solve, then order them by severity or immediacy. Which benefits will elicit the most dramatic response?

Remember: prevention is a weak appeal. People are much more willing to pay for a cure to an existing problem.

Onward.

Read your copy out loud

Once you've given your first draft some structure, print the ad and read it aloud. As you read, make notes… cross things out… make changes. If the words don't roll off your tongue, change them.

The first time you do this it will take a while. You'll have to stop and make changes constantly. That's okay. It's part of the process. Just keep going.

Once you've made it all the way through, make the changes on your computer. Then, print it out again and repeat the process until you've done it ten times.

Yes, ten.

By the tenth time, your ad will be as smooth as a baby's bum.

Okay, as you go through the editing process, use the following "tests" to guide you.

The "so what?" test

If the reader can ever say, "so what?" while reading then you've lost them… no second chances.

The "off on a tangent" test

Your ad should take the reader on a greased slide from the headline right through to the order form. If your copy goes off on a tangent, then you'll lose your reader and lose the sale.

"The greased slide"

John Carlton says your prospect should start reading and be rushed at a giddy pace, breathless, from word-to-word, sentence-to-sentence, and paragraph-to-paragraph, until they're so excited they simply can't wait to order your product.

That word—really?!

When you are reviewing your copy, ask yourself, "would I use this word if my life depended on the success of the ad?"

Long Copy Vs. Short Copy

If you will indulge your imagination for a few moments, I will give you the definitive answer to the question, "how long should your copy be?"

Are you ready?

Okay, I want you to imagine it is your job to sell your supplement the president of a large corporation.

You know this man is very stressed and struggles to maintain his energy through the long working day. And you know that your supplement can help boost and sustain his energy levels.

Over the last year, you have sent him seven direct mail letters, followed up with a phone call and email each time.

Now, finally, he has invited you in for a meeting.

This is your one shot to sell your supplement. In the words of Eminem:

"Look. If you had one shot, or one opportunity, to seize everything you ever wanted, in one moment, would you capture it, or just let it slip?"

You'd capture it, wouldn't you? You'd try to bond with him. You'd ask him questions. You'd try to paint a picture in his mind of how his life would improve if he had more energy. You'd introduce your product and answer his questions. And, you'd give him as much information as he needed to make a buying decision.

How long would that take you—from the introductory handshake to signing on the dotted line?

30 minutes?

45 minutes?

An hour?

Two hours?

Or would it depend?

Of course it would. It would depend on how many questions he had, whether he'd tried a similar supplement before and whether it had worked or not.

It would depend on how easy it was for him to understand how your product worked, the offer, and the guarantee.

Simply, if this was your one shot at making the sale, you would not be stupid enough to give yourself an arbitrary, self-imposed time restriction.

And there's your answer to the question of brevity in advertising…

As Long As It Takes To Make The Sale!

Remember, advertising is simply salesmanship multiplied by a mass medium.

If you wouldn't restrict your selling time in-person, why would you do so in your ad?

It's not a case of "the longer the better", it's simply that your ad must tell a complete story, which may take three paragraphs... or... it may take 60 pages.

You know, I remember hearing Dan Kennedy recall the time when Fred Herman—America's greatest sales trainer—appeared on The Tonight Show with Johnny Carson.

Apparently, Carson challenged Herman: "Since you're such a great salesman, sell me this ashtray."

Fred picked the ashtray up and replied: "If you were going to buy this ashtray, what you would expect to pay for it?"

Carson named a price....

... and Fred replied: **"Sold!"**

What an incredible demonstration.

But even Fred Herman couldn't sell everything as quickly as he "sold" the ashtray. He'd need more time to sell some products, I'm sure.

But still, long-form copy is looked upon as some kind of dirty, aged approach to advertising.

There's some truth in this: people won't read ads that bore them. They won't read ads for entertainment. And they won't read ads whose subject does not interest them.

In other words, they don't want information for the sake of information.

Customers love long copy when it's all about their passions.

They are hurting. They want an alternative to drugs. They want to put an end to the pain. They want guidance, direction and enough information to be convinced to give your product a try.

In fact, people will read several pages of advertising and then ask for a book with even MORE information.

What About Online, Though?

In every single emergence of new media in advertising, there was a chorus of "long copy won't work for this." And in every case, it wasn't so. And it's true online. You're there to sell something. Your ad is your salesman. And long copy works because it's necessary to fit in all the elements of a killer sales pitch—regardless of the media.

Here is how to make your copy read like a "can't put it down" novel...

Use "Reason Why" Copy.

The best way to grip your read for long periods is to use "reason why" copy.

Explain everything you say using good, catchy, believable reasons that convince the reader.

Reason why copy helps you avoid bragging without backing it up.

Here are some ways to use "reason why" copy...

"Here's what it's all about…"

"Here's how to order…"

"Here's why I'm telling you this…"

"Here's the deal…"

"Here's what this product will do for you…"

A Crash Course In Direct Response Design

I'll always remember John Carlton—"the most ripped-off writer on the web"—telling a story about one of his first freelance jobs with a Los Angeles ad agency.

The job was to write a one-page sales letter from an insurance company to cold leads, and the client had already rejected the first four attempts the agency had made.

Overnight, Carlton wrote a sales letter that the Vice President of the agency and the insurance company both loved.

Then, he was asked to sit in a room with an agency designer to "work it out".

Turns out, the designer immediately told Carlton he had to cut several paragraphs of copy to fit in with the layout she had already designed.

She had included several "dumb" images, and the small remaining area was where the copy had to "fit".

Despite being the new kid on the block at the time, Carlton knew something she didn't: the purpose of direct response marketing is to make the sale…. and…

It's Not Design That Sells The Product... It's The Copy That Sells The Product!

So, his response was that "you don't cut the copy to fit the design. You redo the design to accommodate the copy".

Wise words.

However, although the copy is most certainly king, design is still very important.

You see, great design helps the copy do it's selling job even better, and therefore increases response. Bad design, on the other hand, can murder response.

Fortunately, you can't go far wrong with this.

Although art and some other types of design are subjective, graphic design for direct response is scientific.

Sales tests have proven, over many years, that certain techniques are more effective at generating response than others.

You know, Clayton Makepeace, the world's highest paid copywriter, wrote a superb blog post about this subject on his website called *Direct Response Graphic Design 101*, and I highly recommend reading it.

That said, here's your crash course in direct response design.

Pretty versus ugly

When I was just getting started as a copywriter, I was introduced to the Director of an advertising agency in the UK.

When I told him I was interested in direct response, he said that most agencies, businesses and copywriters ARE NOT interested.

"How come?", I asked.

After some thought, he replied...

"It's dirty."

I sat there in silence, too stunned to ask why before the conversation moved on.

But on reflection, I think one of the main reasons why direct response gets a bad rap is that...

An ugly layout usually out-pulls a pretty one—often by as much as 20-30%.

You won't find a beautiful direct response ad. At least not beautiful in the conventional sense.

Obviously, that's because businesses savvy to the wealth-building power of direct response are too busy counting their mounds of cash to care whether anybody thinks their advertising is pretty.

But it does beg the question: why does ugly outperform pretty?

Here's what Eugene Schwartz had to say in his terrific Rodale seminar:

"Beauty looks much the same. It has a narrow definition. Ugliness is randomness, which means there are 100 different ways to be ugly and only 2-3 ways to be beautiful. Ugly, in a world of beauty, stands out."

You may not like it. You may say your ad is unattractive, crowded and hard to read. But the tests will prove they sell better… and they pay.

If you're in business to help the people in your market solve a burning problem or desire, then you first have to persuade them to buy. It's your moral and ethical obligation to put your ego aside and do what many years of advertising tests have proven beyond all doubt.

Ugly sells.

Images and artwork

Never sacrifice sales copy for a graphic. Ads are not written to interest, please or amuse. Pictures, therefore, should only be used when they provide a better sales argument than the same amount of space in type.

In fact, the only valid use of illustrations in sales promotions are:

1. To seize the prospect's attention and to convert that attention to readership—like including the author's photograph with a headline

2. To establish credibility—using charts, graphs, tables or photos of a source to prove a point… or to make a testimonial believable by including a photo of the customer

3. To drive important sales points home—"before/after" photos, "process photos" showing how the product works, etc.

4. To present the product and/or premium in a way that enhances its perceived value.

If you choose to include artwork, here are some guidelines to maximize profitability.

Don't spend too much

Tests prove that good quality artwork pays as well as mediocre. So, you can make your point without spending a lot. Increasing the quality beyond mediocre will not increase response. The appeal lies in the subject.

Make it relevant

An eccentric or unique picture takes attention from the subject. General attention is useless—it should be focused on the main appeal, reflected in your headline. Remember: the picture must help sell the product.

Think carefully about color

If the only reason to use a color picture is to gain attention, interest, or amuse... then don't do it.

Only use color if it does a better job of placing the product on real exhibition, like it might for food items —oranges and deserts, for example.

If there is no difference in cost, then it may make sense to just use color.

Use the same picture in repeat ads

Once you've found a picture that does a good selling job, by all means, use it in repeat ads. It's a mistake to assume anyone will see it twice. The odds are very low. And even if they do, repetition does not retract; it drives the sales message home.

Photographs over illustrations

The late Bill Jayme, who wrote many successful direct mail health packages, said that photographs pull better than illustrations. They should create a vision in the prospect's mind of the promise of what their life will be like after using your product... or demonstrate how a product achieves that.

A good picture example

In his book *Scientific Advertising*, Claude Hopkins said that images of puffed grains were extremely effective. They aroused curiosity in the product, so people responded with orders.

Salesmanship multiplied

Remember that advertising is just salesmanship multiplied by a mass medium.

Artwork in ads is like the clothes of a salesman; they are not too important. Some poorly dressed men are great salespeople. Overdress in either is a fault.

Type size

In health markets, many of your prospects are older and may struggle to read small copy. If they need to fetch their glasses to read your pitch, then the chance of them buying is greatly reduced. As a result, body copy should never be smaller than 12pt. and you might even consider using 14pt. type.

Be aware, though, that there is a point of diminishing returns.

Bigger copy takes up more space. If you make the copy bigger than it needs to be then you are paying more for each sale.

Mail order tests have proven beyond doubt that if you double your type size, and double the space, then you are paying double the price for sales.

Keep your typical buyer in mind. Make the copy big enough to read with glasses, but not so big that you pay more for the space than you need to. 12pt. or 14pt. is good for most ads.

Your headline and subheads are a different matter altogether. Their purpose is to seize the reader's attention, and larger and bolder heads generally seize attention better than smaller, lighter ones.

Typeface

Sans-serif type tends to be easier to read online. In print, though, readership studies show that serif type is far more readable. That's why most newspapers and magazines use Times for their body copy.

Layout

A few pointers on layout from Clayton Makepeace, from his graphic design post referenced above:

• "Full-page sidebars on right-hand pages create a visual barrier and can discourage the reader from turning the page

• "Subheads should never be broken between columns, and when near the bottom of a column, should always have at least three lines of text beneath them

• "Subheads should be broken into coherent phrases

• "Justified text—where both the left- and right-hand margin of each paragraph is even—destroys readership

• "A widow—a single word on the last line of a paragraph—is usually a good thing. It adds a smidgen of white space, making the page look less intimidating

• "Orphans—the single line of a new paragraph at the bottom of the column—should be avoided. It breaks a thought before it can take hold in the prospect's mind"

• "At the end of the text on each page, insert a page-turner: A small "please turn …" flush right."

Color

The human eye likes contrast. The lower the contrast between your text and your background, the lower your readership will be.

As a rule, just stick to black ink on white paper. Or black type on a white background online. Each step you take away from black on white cuts readership.

For sidebars, add a background for separation, but only use a light color—yellow, blue or green— keeping the body text black.

Again, the rules are different for headlines, subheads and other attention-getting copy. You can use color to grab the attention of the reader and bring them into the ad.

Next comes the question, what color?

Most psychologists say that cold colors (like blue) are relaxing. Hotter colors (like red) warm us up. In advertising, we are trying to get prospects excited about ordering, so it generally makes sense to use warmer colors.

Having said that, Clayton Makepeace reports that "junk mail blue" often works well, too. And some of his most successful health promotions used a strong green as a second color.

I guess the only sensible approach is to stick to warm colors until such a time arrives when it makes sense to test different ones.

Sentence and paragraph length

Have you ever looked at a piece of writing and decided not to read because it looked like hard work?

When this happens, it's usually because the writing contains long sentences, long paragraphs, and narrow margins. It looks overwhelming before you even start reading. That's not good for an ad, is it?

The solution is to do everything in your power— and it's not that difficult—to make your ad look immediately attractive to read.

One way to do that is to use short sentences. If you can, use short line lengths too. This is easier if you are using columns. Columns allow the eye and brain to read and interpret a few words at a time, then quickly move on to the next line.

Also, use short paragraphs. Don't be afraid of breaking paragraphs in places that would drive the grammar Nazi's berserk.

Best: don't use any very long paragraphs but vary the length a little to provide eye relief.

How To Know If You Have A Winner Without Spending A Dime

My very first sales letter was sent to 25 local businesses, promoting my copywriting services.

And stapled to the top of each letter was a real lottery ticket.

Here's how the lead read:

"Local Advertising Copywriter Writes Simple Ads That Increase Customer Base For North Devon Businesses

Dear NAME,

I attached a Thunderball ticket to this letter to get your attention (and hopefully make you a millionaire in the process!). Here's why:"

Now that you've seen the lead, can you guess how well this letter pulled?

I'll tell you: I got no business whatsoever.

Not just because of the quality of the copy (which makes me cringe), but my choice of market was terrible.

Most local businesses, especially where I lived at the time, had no idea what a copywriter was, let alone what copywriting could do for their business. In other words...

They Weren't Buying What I Was Selling!

Big mistake.

Anyway, that's not the point of this story. What I want to share with you came a little later.

See, a week after I'd sent the letter off in the hands of Mr. Postman, I phoned each one of the 25 prospects on my list.

If and when I got through to the relevant person, the conversation went something like this:

"Mr. Jones?"

"Yes. How can I help?"

"Hi. My name is Callum Birch. I sent you a letter with a lottery ticket attached. Did you receive it?"

"Yes, yes I did. Thank you for your letter. Very clever marketing idea... but I don't have any need for your services at the moment. Thanks anyway."

Ouch.

"Very clever marketing idea"

Those words will be etched into my brain until the day I die.

"Clever"—just what I was going for!

Do you see the point? Despite what many marketing people will tell you, the purpose of a sales letter is not to make a good impression or to show how clever you are or show off your writing style. No, no, no...

It's To Make The Damn Sale!

I couldn't afford to keep sending letters which business owners' thought were "clever". In fact, I couldn't afford to send ANY more letters.

And that was only 25... the risk only increases as the number of letters increases. But you know what? This experience taught me a hell of a lot about marketing. And, there's something in here (yes, I'm getting to the point) that directly applies to you.

You see, it doesn't matter what anybody else thinks of your copy. It doesn't matter what your spouse thinks. It doesn't matter what your boss thinks. And yes, to an extent, it doesn't matter what your client thinks. The only person whose reaction to your letter matters is...

Somebody In Your Market!

Notice how I used the word "reaction". That was deliberate. You see, I could have said it's the "opinion" of your market that matters. But it's not, because you're not looking for an advertising critique. No, when reviewing your copy, what you want to know is...

Whether They Will Put Their Hand In Their Pocket And Pull Out Their Cold Hard Cash For Your Product!

A case in point: the late great Gary Halbert used to go to a bar full of prospects for the book he was selling.

He would ask a guy at the bar to read his ad. And, if they reacted by complimenting his writing, or asking him to explain it some more, then he knew he had a loser.

But if the guy said he'd really like a copy of the book and asked Halbert how to get ahold of one, then the Price of Print knew he had a winner.

Can you see the power of this technique? I'll lay it out for you:

• Find somebody in your market (perhaps someone you spoke to during research)

• Send them a copy of your ad (but don't tell them it's yours or they'll give you an advertising critique— just say, "I found this and thought you'd find it interesting")

• Go back to them a few days later and ask, "what did you think of that letter?"

If they say something like: "I tried to order it, but the link didn't work" or "Do you know how I can get this?" ...

… then you know your ad has a good chance of succeeding.

But, if you get any other reaction, if they seem lethargic or uninterested, you know you've missed something.

Then, you can go back to the drawing board and figure out how to improve it.

Here's the kicker: you can do ALL of this before you or your client invest in your ad… and… without spending a dime!

PART V:
FTC & FDA
COMPLIANCE

Why You Should Ignore The FDA And The FTC

If you want to write supplement ads for your own products or your clients, then you'll need to familiarize yourself with basic FTC and FDA advertising principles.

Why?

Well, the most obvious reason is that an ad which breaks FTC or FDA rules could land you in the slammer.

Plus, the media love to attack supplement companies, so the knock-on effect of an FTC investigation could be disastrous.

And... if you're still willing to take the risk... let me tell you one more reason why you should do your level best to play by the rules.

It's really a rather simple reason. You see, the FTC just wants to make sure your advertising is truthful and not misleading. In other words...

Breaking FTC Rules Means Lying To Your Customers!

And why, oh why, would you want to do that?

Okay, before we get into the nitty-gritty, a word of caution.

There's a very good reason I put this section near the end of the book. You see, if you worry about legalities too early in the process of writing copy then one of two things will happen:

1. You'll get the dreaded writer's block, or

2. You'll write an ad with less substance than Kim Kardashian

While it's your professional responsibility to understand the regulations and do what you can to help your client comply, your real job is to write kickass copy that pulls in orders!

Simply focus on writing passionate, convincing copy—and then tone down the claims in the review process if needs be.

The best approach is to pretend that the FTC and FDA do not even exist while you are writing the ad. Go all in. Tell the truth, no bars hold. Say what needs to be said to make the sale.

Then, and only then, work with your client's attorney to make sure it's compliant.

It's much easier to tone down your copy to make it compliant than it is to give flat copy an energy boost.

That being said, you can save yourself and your client a lot of time and grief by developing a basic understanding of FTC and FDA regulations.

After all, you will have to work with them to figure out how to make the ad compliant, after their attorney's hand back your first draft with a bunch of compliance issues.

What The FTC Has To Say

Ready for your crash course in FTC regulations?

I'll try and keep it interesting…but frankly… it's a dull subject, so no promises.

What I can guarantee is that I'll dispose of the legalese and only give you what you need to know.

Right, here are the four laws and organizations you are governed by…

1. First, there's the Dietary Supplement Health and Education Act of 1994 (DSHEA), which states that nutritional supplement products must follow specific labeling rules

2. Next, there's the U.S. Food and Drug Administration (FDA). The FDA is responsible for implementing DSHEA. They govern product labeling, including packaging inserts and other point-of-sale promotional material

3. The Federal Trade Commission (FTC) govern advertising CLAIMS and have specific rules and guidelines for nutritional supplement advertisers

4. Finally, every state in the US has consumer protection laws that govern advertising independently from the FTC and FDA

Unfortunately, I can't help you with state-specific laws. There's just too many, and I'm not an attorney.

The FDA governs product labeling so, whilst I cover their rules briefly, labeling isn't the focus of this book.

What You Really Need To Know About Are The FTC Guidelines.

Why? Because the FTC govern advertising claims. And as a copywriter, you are responsible for writing an ad that makes those claims. Here's what the FTC has to say, in a nutshell:

1. Advertising must be truthful and not misleading

2. Before disseminating an ad, advertisers must have adequate substantiation for all objective product claims

That applies to ALL advertising in the U.S., so let's dig in and see if we can't apply this specifically to nutritional supplements.

How To Tell If Your Ad Is FTC Compliant

There's no point in sending you to sleep by regurgitating the FTC guidelines. So, let's get right into how to apply the FTC guidelines to your ad and make it a compliant.

First things first, the FTC cannot review and clear ads in advance of publication. It's on you and your team (or your client's team).

Actually, it's ultimately up to your attorney, but the rest of this section should make you a much more useful partner.

Now, when the FTC catch wind of suspicious ad, they launch an investigation. Specifically, they follow this four-step process:

1. Identify all "express" and "implied" claims

2. Determine what the ad does NOT say—but should

3. Decide whether each claim is important to the consumer's decision to buy or use the product

4. Investigate whether there is sufficient evidence to substantiate each claim.

Why am I telling you this?

Well, it seems to me that—when it comes to reviewing the copy with your client or attorney—you might as well just use the FTC's process yourself!

Can't really go wrong then, can you?

Let's talk about each of those steps in more detail.

The Two Types Of Claim You Need To Back Up

There are two types of advertising claim: express and implied.

An express claim is one made directly in the ad, such as: "ABC mouthwash prevents colds."

An implied claim is one that is made indirectly or by inference: "ABC Mouthwash kills the germs that cause colds."

This implies that the product will prevent colds.

Sometimes even a short sentence can contain both express and implied claims. You must be able to back them BOTH up.

For example: "90% of cardiologists take the vitamin supplement."

Express claim: 90% of cardiologists are using the supplement.

Implied claim: the product offers some benefit to the heart.

In this case, the advertiser must be able to substantiate both of these claims. Here's another example:

"University studies prove that a mineral supplement can improve athletic performance."

Express claim: "university studies prove."

Implied claim: the studies are methodologically sound. The advertiser must have access to the university studies AND prove that they are methodologically sound (more on that later).

Now, in supplement advertising, all of your express and implied claims must have objective evidence to support them.

What if your product is relatively new to the market?

Well, the FTC is flexible to some extent. You can advertise products with an emerging body of evidence, but it has to be robust enough that the information and claims in your ad are accurate.

So, start the review process by identifying all of the individual express and implied claims. Then, consider the ad as a whole, and assess the "net impression" conveyed by all elements.

Treat These Claims With Caution

Consumer watchdog groups have identified these words as potential indicators of fraudulent supplement claims: natural, miracle, magic, detoxify, energize, breakthrough, safe, purify.

You don't need to avoid them entirely but *be careful*. Define them. Back them up. Let your prospects know what you mean by the term.

Further, here are seven health claims which have been "flagged up" as over-the-top:

1. Causes weight loss of two pounds or more a week for a month or two without dieting or exercise

2. Causes substantial weight loss no matter what or how much the consumer eats

3. Causes permanent weight loss (even when the consumer stops using the product)

4. Blocks the absorption of fat or calories to enable consumers to lose substantial weight

5. Safely enables consumers to lose more than three pounds per week for more than four weeks

6. Causes substantial weight loss for all users

7. Causes substantial weight loss by wearing it on the body or rubbing it into the skin.

The lesson is simple: don't make claims like these. It's quite clear that they can't be backed up.

Not only will they make your advertising ineffective, but if you or your client insist on making claims that deceive your customer's, then I dare say you won't be in business for long.

How To Back Your Claims

Substantiating ("backing up") your claims usually requires competent and reliable scientific evidence.

And, if a particular claim or your ad as a whole lends itself to more than one reasonable interpretation, you are responsible for substantiating them all.

At a minimum, you must have the level of support that you claim to have in the ad—either expressly or by implication.

A word of caution: The FTC is particularly interested in unsubstantiated claims that could lead consumers to forego other treatments which have been validated by scientific evidence... or to self-medicate for serious conditions without medical supervision.

I'm sure you wouldn't deliberately consider misleading people like this (although there are scumbags who do), but it is certainly possible to get carried away in your enthusiasm for your product and do this accidentally.

Unfortunately, the effect on the consumer is the same, and potentially life-threatening... so... be careful.

Check your endorsements, too.

At a certain point in the compliance review process, you might be tempted to make up for the watering down of claims using endorsements from customers or experts.

Before you get too excited, claims made by endorser's are treated in the same vein as claims made anywhere else in the ad—they must have appropriate scientific evidence to back them up.

Expert endorsers must have appropriate qualifications as an expert—and must have conducted an examination or testing of the product generally accepted in the field to be sufficient to support the claim.

And finally, if there is a material connection between the endorser and advertiser, then it must be disclosed. This includes personal, financial or other connections that the consumer wouldn't reasonably expect.

How To Substantiate Testimonials

Statements, testimonials and case studies of satisfied customers are not sufficient to support health claims.

Nor are money-back guarantees.

In fact, claims made in testimonials or case studies must be substantiated in the same manner as claims made in the rest of the ad.

Testimonials about the efficacy or safety of a supplement should be backed by adequate substantiation that the experience represents what other consumers will generally achieve.

Otherwise, you include a clear and conspicuous disclaimer. "Results may vary" is not enough. Either explain what the generally expected results are… or… tell the consumer in no uncertain terms that they should not expect the same results.

What To Do If Your Claims Are Based On Historical Use

It is possible to back up claims based on their historical or traditional use. But in this case, the claims must be either:

1. Substantiated by scientific evidence, or

2. Presented in such a way that the reader understands that the basis for the claim is the historical use of the product for a particular purpose.

In other words, if there is no scientific evidence to support the claims, you should make sure the ad doesn't imply that there is.

And, claims based on documented historical must be relevant to its historic use—in administration, formulation of ingredients, and dose.

How To Avoid Misleading Your Customers

Earlier in this section, I mentioned that the FTC says that advertising must be truthful and not misleading.

What does that mean, exactly?

Well, the FTC defines ads that break this rule as "deceptive". Simply, deceptive ads are those which:

1. Contain a misrepresentation or omission which is likely to mislead consumers acting reasonably under the circumstances

2. Important to a consumer's decision to buy or use the product

Misrepresentations

An ad may contain a misrepresentation if it makes a claim that cannot be substantiated.

Similarly, an advertiser might be able to back up a claim to a certain extent... but... if a stronger body of evidence runs contrary to the claimed effect, then even a qualified claim is likely to be deceptive.

Omissions

An ad can also be deceptive for its failure to say something. If it would be misleading without certain qualifying information, that information must be disclosed. Example of missing information:

'Mineral supplement claims it can eliminate a specific deficiency that causes fatigue.'

In reality, less than 2% of the audience suffered from deficiency. The advertiser should, therefore, have disclosed this information so that consumers understood the fact that only a small percentage were likely to experience fatigue reduction.

How to handle potential side effects

Some supplements, particularly those containing herbs, have known side effects… often when used in conjunction with medication.

If you don't disclose potential side effects, not only will you mislead your prospect and break the law, you'll also endanger their health.

"But if I disclose the side effects… NOBODY will buy!"

Not true.

In fact, the best way to deal with side effects is to very clearly and unambiguously warn people in the copy, on the packaging, etc.

If a problem occurs when used in combination with some other drug, you really don't want those people to buy.

And… and…

Your honesty and transparency will only make other prospects MORE likely to buy!

What Counts As Evidence?

Next up, the FTC says that health claims must be supported by "competent and reliable scientific evidence—evaluated by people qualified to review it."

What, exactly, qualifies as "competent and reliable scientific evidence"?

Well, scientific evidence includes tests, analyses, research, studies, and other types of evidence based on the expertise of professionals in the research area.

As for "competent and reliable" ... that's a little harder to define. But here are some guidelines.

Quality over quantity

Quality is more important than quantity. One study with reliable and conclusive findings carries much more weight than 100 flawed studies (surprisingly common).

Look for control

A study carefully controlled, with blinding of subjects and researchers, is likely to yield more reliable results.

A double-blind, place-controlled trial is usually considered the gold standard.

The longer the better

A study of longer duration can provide better evidence that the claimed effect will persist... and... it will help resolve potential safety questions.

Beware the placebo effect

Statistical significance of findings is important. Non-significant results may mean that the measured effects are due to the placebo effect or chance.

Researchers should always report on statistical significance in their publication. And, note that the results must be enough to translate into a meaningful benefit for consumers—not so small they have only a trivial effect.

Replication

The replication of research results in an independently-conducted study adds to the weight of evidence.

Other types of evidence

When a clinical trial is not possible, epidemiological evidence may be an acceptable substitute—especially when supported by other evidence.

Failing that, results from animal and in-vitro studies may be used... but only if they are widely considered an acceptable substitute for human research (or where human research is not possible).

Finally, unpublished work can be also considered… but… the publication of a peer-reviewed study suggests the research has been subject to a level of scrutiny so will always carry more weight.

What to do when evidence is lacking

If the effect of your supplement has an emerging body of science (like CBD oil, at the time of writing) but the evidence is insufficient to substantiate a claim, then make sure your audience understand the extent of scientific support and the existence of any significant contradictory evidence.

Consider the whole

Finally, do not evaluate studies in isolation or only use positive evidence when there exists contradictory evidence.

Wide variation in outcomes of studies and inconsistent/conflicting results raise serious questions about the adequacy of a substantiation.

What to do when studies conflict

If studies are inconsistent—ask how relevant each piece of research is to the claim… the strengths and weaknesses of each study… and look first to the results of studies with the most reliable methodologies.

Go beyond the abstract

An abstract or informal summary is written to give you an overview of a research study, but it never gives you enough information about how the study was conducted, or its limitations, to decide whether it can be used to substantiate your claims.

Use the abstract to quickly decide if a study might be relevant, then go deeper.

Relevance

The evidence you use must be high quality but, in order to substantiate your advertising claims, it must also support the specific claims in your ad.

In other words, you must be able to point to evidence that backs-up each specific claim, not just a broader claim.

Four questions to determine whether evidence is relevant to a specific claim:

1. How does the dosage/formulation advertise compare to what was used in the study?

2. Does the product contain additional ingredients that might alter the effect proven by the studies?

3. Is the product administered in the same manner as in the study?

4. Does the study population reflect the characteristics and lifestyle of the population targeted by the ad?

How To Write An FDA-Compliant Product Disclaimer

Under DSHEA, statements of nutritional support for dietary supplements must be accompanied by a two-part disclaimer on the product label which states that:

1. The statement has not been evaluated by the FDA

2. The product is not intended to diagnose, treat, cure or prevent any disease

Although DSHEA does not govern advertising, there are situations where such a disclosure should be used in your advertisement and product labeling to prevent consumers from being misled about the nature of the product... and... the extent to which regulatory authorities have reviewed its efficacy and safety.

For example, if the copy or images in your ad might lead consumers to believe the product has been reviewed to the same extent as the FDA examines new drugs—and that it has been found to be beneficial for the treatment of disease—then disclosure may be necessary.

Otherwise, the advertisement would be considered deceptive.

So that's the ad itself and your product labeling… what about other marketing materials?

Well, if you use independently written literature, scientific journal articles, books, and other publications in the sales process… they must also comply with the FTC.

However, assuming they do comply and are not misleading, you don't have to add labeling to them.

How to write disclosures

You must present qualifying information clearly and predominantly—so it's actually noticed and understood by consumers. Fine print and buried disclosures are not adequate. Disclosures must also:

• Use clear language

• Avoid small type

• Avoid inconsistent statements

• Avoid distracting elements

• Be presented near to the claims to which they apply

Basically, be completely transparent and don't try to bury or hide the truth—even if you think it will affect sales.

Your Role And Responsibilities In The Compliance Process

Jeez, this section has been boring, hasn't it?

To tell you the truth, I've had about as much fun writing as I expect you've had reading. But as I said at the start of the chapter...

If you are or want to be a nutritional supplements copywriter, swatting up on the FTC and how it affects your client will make you a much stronger ally.

And, if you sell your own supplement products, it is absolutely critical that you know how to comply with the FTC and FDA guidelines

To that end, here are a few more things to bear in mind.

Every time I begin working with a client, I ask them to rate where they stand on regulations on a 1-10 scale.

This gives me an idea of their comfort zone so I can avoid wasting my time (and theirs) on writing an ad they will never go for.

Carline Cole, the prolific health copywriter, takes this a step further. On her website, Carline actively discourages prospective clients from contacting her if they aren't comfortable with ballsy copy like she wrote for her many controls.

However you decide to approach this, just bear in mind that your first and primary job is to write copy that pulls in orders.

This is in direct conflict with the role of your client's attorney (or your own), whose job it is to prevent lawsuits.

More.

Remember to keep hard copies of all your sources, and a version of your promotion that includes citations, including research your client sent you.

And, make sure all testimonials and case studies are documented and signed by the people who gave them.

Finally, I have a disclosure of my own: **I am NOT an attorney**.

What you are reading here is my own interpretation of FTC and FDA guidelines as they apply to nutritional supplements advertising.

You should not use them to confirm the compliance of your advertising. Use a qualified attorney to do that.

In fact, I don't take any responsibility for the compliance of my client's advertising… and… neither should you.

Make sure there's a clause in your contract that says you'll make every effort to stay compliant, but that you cannot be held legally responsible for the promotion.

Okay, that's a wrap!

PART VI:

RESOURCES

Free Daily Email Tips

If you want to learn more about writing white hot nutritional supplement copy, then head on over to *callumbirch.com.*

You'll find hundreds of advanced marketing tips, including:

• How to write copy for magalogs, packaging and emails

• Copywriter horror stories (how one well-known marketer got duped out of $10k)

• Why your backend is where the real money is

• How to combine online and offline media to boost profits

There's so much to know about nutritional supplement copywriting that I couldn't possibly squeeze everything into this book.

So, I decided to publish daily emails. Yes, DAILY! …

… and my goal is simple: to pack every email with entertaining but deadly serious information on nutritional supplement copywriting that...

You can apply today and profit from tomorrow!

Gobble it up at *callumbirch.com.*

Resources

Books

How to Write Irresistible Copy for Nutritional Supplements, by Sarah Clachar and Bob Bly

Scientific Advertising, by Claude Hopkins

Tested Advertising Methods, by John Caples

How to Write a Good Advertisement, by Victor Schwab

The Robert Collier Letter Book, by Robert Collier

The Ultimate Sales Letter, by Dan Kennedy

Ready, Fire, Aim: Zero to $100 Million in No Time Flat, by Michael Masterson

A Technique for Producing Ideas, by James Webb Young

Ogilvy on Advertising, by David Ogilvy

Breakthrough Advertising, by Eugene Schwartz

Great Leads, by Michael Masterson and John Forde

Websites

The Total Package by Clayton Makepeace: makepeacetotalpackage.com

The Gary Halbert Letter by Gary Halbert: thegaryhalbertletter.com

American Writer's & Artists Inc. (AWAI): awai.com

Guides

FTC Guidelines Advertising FAQ's: A Guide for Small Business, Federal Trade Commission (FTC)

Dietary Supplements: An Advertising Guide for Industry, Federal Trade Commission (FTC)

Voluntary Guidelines for Providers of Weight Loss Products or Services, Federal Trade Commission (FTC)

About The Author

Callum Birch is a direct marketing consultant and copywriter who specializes in nutritional supplement promotions.

In a past life, Callum worked as a healthcare professional for 6 years. In that time, he cared for over 6600 patients—mostly baby boomers—and developed a deep understanding of what motivates the 50+ health-conscious consumer.

Callum also has a master's degree in health research, which helps him find unique angles other copywriter's miss... and... generate a higher response by using scientific evidence to *prove* advertising claims (and avoid dreaded FTC investigations).

You can contact Callum at:

92 Pilton Street, Barnstaple, Devon EX311PQ, United Kingdom

Phone: +44(0) 1271 374 081

Email: callum@callumbirch.com

NOTE: Callum responds to communications as quickly as possible. However, he is very busy, so please allow ample time for a response. Further, please communicate sparingly about one subject at a time. Thank you.

www.ingramcontent.com/pod-product-compliance
Lightning Source LLC
Chambersburg PA
CBHW051207170526
45158CB00014B/1389